HERALDRY, ANCESTRY AND TITLES

QUESTIONS AND ANSWERS

HERALDRY, ANCESTRY and TITLES

Questions and Answers

BY

L. G. PINE

B.A. Lond. Barrister-at-Law, Inner Temple,
F.S.A. Scot., F.J.I., F.A.M.S.
Formerly Editor of Burke's Peerage
and of Burke's Landed Gentry, etc., etc.

Gramercy Publishing Company
New York

Contents

Chapter 1. Heraldry

5

Contents

Contents

Chapter 2. Ancestors

Contents

Contents

Chapter 3. Titles

9

Contents

Contents

Contents

12

List of Illustrations

13

Introduction

I have had thirty years' experience with these subjects which includes twenty-five years' connection with *Burke's Peerage, Burke's Landed Gentry,* and the other genealogical books associated with the name of Burke. During the greater part of that time I was the Editor of these publications and as such I received some very varied and remarkable questions and requests. When putting an epitaph on a peer's tombstone, should one put, in addition to his title, his surname, or his Christian names only? How does one get one's obituary into *The Times*? Was the name of William the Conqueror's mother Charlotte Skinner? Is the Queen styled Duchess of Normandy? Can anyone get a coat of arms? What is the Roll of Battle Abbey? How many people in England can prove Norman descent? Can the Queen deprive a peer of his title?

This is only a selection of questions which have been put to me, sometimes at lectures or over the telephone, or in letters. I continue to receive a huge correspondence from all over the world, which is addressed to me, about fifty per cent. to my home, the rest care of publishers, agents and newspapers, and at times simply to L. G. Pine, Author (or Genealogist), England.

This volume of correspondence and inquiry bears witness to a widespread interest in the subjects of heraldry, ancestry, titles and peerage. Yet in very many cases the inquirers have tried to find the answers elsewhere, in books or other sources, and have failed, largely, I think, because the official custodians of knowledge are not sufficiently aware of the outlook of the ordinary man or woman. I have had the great advantage of personal contact in over 600 lectures and through some thousands of letters, so that in writing on these subjects I am able to envisage real persons who have asked real questions.

The illustrations are by W. J. Hill.

1

Heraldry

1. In the first place what is heraldry?

It is a system of the use of hereditary symbols handed down in families or in institutions. It originated in western Europe about the middle of the twelfth century. The correct term should be armoury, for the real meaning of heraldry is the 'art or office of a herald'. In course of time heraldry has come to be the term used to cover the science and art of these hereditary symbols or coats of arms.

2. What is a crest?

A crest is part of a coat of arms. It was fixed on to the top of the helmet of the knight in armour. It is perfectly possible to have a genuine coat of arms without a crest, but not to have a crest without a coat of arms. (It is true that there is one case recorded at the College of Arms of a man for whom only a crest is recorded. It is improbable that many people will want to imitate this example for the man in question died when his crest was approved and before the rest of the coat of arms was passed.)

3. Why then is the term 'crest' used so frequently instead of the correct term 'coat of arms'?

Pure ignorance, as Dr. Johnson said of his definition of the word 'pastern'. On one occasion I was awakened at

1 a.m. by an unfortunate journalist who was forced in the still watches to wrestle with what he called the problem of Earl Mountbatten's 'crest'. Next morning I had the great satisfaction of reading for once the correct description of the arms as a coat of arms.

For reasons of space, crests have been used on small objects such as spoons or other silver ware, on motor-cars, rings, livery buttons, notepaper, etc., often in conjunction with the family motto, but without the full coat of arms which would have been more bulky to engrave. Hence the idea has arisen in popular speech of a crest as synonymous with a coat of arms.

There are, in fact, four terms which are correct usage, these being, coat of arms, armorial bearings, heraldic achievement or shield. The last named is somewhat poetic. It occurs (usually quite wrongly) in Tennyson's 'Idylls of the King'. Most of the notable English writers are at sea on the subject of heraldry, though William Shakespeare is a great exception. He was, however, an arrant snob and spent three years trying to get a coat of arms. He succeeded and so was able to be described as 'gent', on his funeral monument.

Suffice to add that no one who understands the rudiments of Heraldry refers to a crest other than in its proper usage as part of a coat of arms. 'Crest' in the wrong sense is paralleled by 'bar sinister' (see below) which again is frequently used in popular writing to denote bastardy.

4. Is there a coat of arms for every name?

No. This idea is much the same with the belief that every Scottish family is entitled to wear a tartan. There are a very large number of coats of arms in existence, about 100,000 being included in *Burke's General Armoury*, but these have all been either (1) granted to the bearers or (2) assumed by them. There is not, however, such a thing as a crest for every surname.

5. What is the bar sinister?

There is no such thing in heraldry. 'Bar sinister' is a popular phrase much used by novelists with whom it probably originated. By them it is used as an expression denoting illegitimacy. 'He started life with the bar sinister on his shield' is the common remark in novels, meaning that the man in question was a bastard. There is a term in French heraldry – *barre sinistre* – which is a translation of the English heraldic term, bend sinister. The French *'barre'* translates 'bend' but it is not the equivalent of the English 'bar'. 'Sinister' in heraldry has no unpleasant connotation but is simply a term of Latin origin which means 'left', and is the opposite of 'dexter' – right. What about the bend sinister? Has some mistake been made and is this the sign of bastardy which the popular writers have mistaken in their bar sinister? No, although a bend sinister has sometimes been used to denote illegitimacy, it is merely one of the marks or charges on a coat of arms, a band which runs from the top left corner of the shield down to the bottom right.

It should be added that a baton sinister is often used as a sign of bastardy. This is particularly the case with royal bastards, and anyone who looks at the arms of the Dukes of Buccleuch, of Grafton, or of St. Albans will see the baton sinister 'debruising' the royal arms of the original duke's father.* It may not be out of place here to mention the subject of royal bastards which may be placed under the form of the following question.

6. Are the bulk of the peers descended from royal bastards?

The answer is an emphatic no. Many English sovereigns did have by-blows, children born on the wrong side of the

---

* 'Debruising' sounds pretty bad, but has nothing to do with any bruising. It merely means a mark or baton set right across the royal arms.

blanket. Charles II is usually debited with twelve bastards, from whom have descended some of our modern peerage. The Earl of Munster is derived from William IV. The winner in the royal bastard stakes was Henry I. Nineteen of his illegitimate offspring are known. Robert Duke of Gloucester who is buried in St. James's Church, Bristol, is the most notable, but no particular mark has been left on the peerage by the exploits of Henry Beauclerk (Henry I's nickname).

The majority of our peers are descended from nothing more exciting than the less competent politicians of the eighteenth century or the more successful business magnates of the industrial revolution.

Strange as it may seem, there are many more legitimate than spurious descendants of our royalty. It has been said that every middle-class Englishman is descended from Edward III. This does not mean that in addition to his foreign conquests, Edward was prodigiously active at home. It is simply that his family survived the rigours of medieval upbringing and lived to have children of their own. The descendants of these were not married within their own royal circle, but gradually spread throughout the whole nation. Today there are known to be some 100,000 persons descended legitimately from Edward III.

It is a comforting thought too, that this king is a kind of genealogical Clapham Junction. Get to him and you are on to the main lines of most of the royalties of the Middle Ages.

7. What other way is there in heraldry of denoting bastardy?

Another way in which heraldic bastardy can be denoted is by the use of the device known as a bordure. This is described as 'an uniform border or edge to a shield, and occupying one fifth of the shield.' It occurs in the coats of arms of some eminent families, but it should not be taken universally as the sign of bastardy. So many Scottish families have it! As my first editor (a Scotsman) remarked, in some of the Highland clans marriage was an institution of late arrival. It appears that during the last two hundred years, the English heralds have got into the habit of using the bordure to signify illegitimacy.

8. Who can get a coat of arms?

It would be rash to exclude anyone from the charitable sweep of the heraldic authorities. Sometimes the question is put in another way; can anyone get a coat of arms? To this I am bound to answer, that I know of no one who has been refused. Of course, no one is likely to apply for a grant, unless he knows what is meant by arms, that is unless he is in a state of grace when arms are the most desirable thing in his mental horizon.

9. How does one obtain a grant?

By applying to the College of Arms (if one lives in England or Wales). The cost is between £140 and £200. It takes usually about a year for the application to be processed through the College. There is an elaborate system of checks and counter-checks. If you are a Scot, you come under the jurisdiction of the Lyon Office in Edinburgh. Heraldry in Scotland is part of the legal system which is distinct from that of England. There is a little difficulty here because people of Scottish descent are supposed to come under Lyon's administration wherever they may be, anywhere in the world; similarly people of English and Welsh descent should look to the English College. There are many variations of these rules. In practice it would be a good thing for each country to have its own heraldic jurisdiction, as it does in everything else. An example where this occurred was in Ireland, where the Republican Government did not like to continue under the heraldic jurisdiction of an official in Dublin whose title was Ulster King of Arms and who was appointed by the British Crown. So an amicable arrangement was reached whereby on the death of Sir Neville Wilkinson in 1940, his post was not filled again at Dublin. Mr. de Valera then appointed his own official with the title, Chief Herald of Ireland, who sits in the old Ulster Office with the Ulster records.

In the meantime the British Crown united the title and office of Ulster King of Arms with that of Norroy King of Arms in the English College, and in practice the Norroy and Ulster King of Arms exercises heraldic control in the province of Ulster, covering the six northern counties. The remaining twenty-six counties of Ireland are in the jurisdiction of the Chief Herald of Ireland. So in theory this means that people of English and Welsh descent wherever they may be should come under the rule of the College of Arms; Scots descended folk under the Lord Lyon; Ulstermen under Norroy and Ulster and republican Irish under the state official in Dublin.

10. You refer to the College of Arms, is this the same as the Heralds' College?

Yes, it is one and the same institution which is located in Queen Victoria Street, London, E.C.4. No one properly acquainted with heraldry refers to Heralds' College; the latter is a colloquialism. The correct term is College of Arms. The Scottish equivalent is: The Lord Lyon, at his Court, H.M. Registry Office, Edinburgh. The Irish office: The Chief Herald of Ireland, Dublin Castle, Dublin, Ireland.

11. When was the College of Arms founded?

In 1484 by King Richard III. There were royal heralds

long before that time, who were members of the royal household. They were formed or consolidated into a College or corporate institution by Richard III.

12. Who are the members of the College of Arms?

There is the head, the Duke of Norfolk, who is hereditary Earl Marshal (i.e. responsible for ceremonial functions such as a Coronation or a royal funeral or the state opening of Parliament). By virtue of his position as Earl Marshal, the Duke presides over the College of Arms.

Under him he has thirteen officers. These are three Kings of Arms: Garter, Clarenceux and Norroy (now combining Ulster). Six Heralds: Windsor, Somerset, York, Lancaster, Chester and Richmond. Four Pursuivants (i.e. followers or junior Heralds): Rouge Dragon, Rouge Croix, Bluemantle, and Portcullis.

The delightful medieval flavour of these names derive partly from the old archaic Norman French language of heraldry, and partly from titles which were connected with the royal family in the reign of Edward III (1327–77).

13. What exactly is the function of the College of Arms?

In a nutshell, it is to look after the use of arms in England and Wales. In past centuries it has had other duties, e.g. the Heralds used at one time to manage the funerals of the nobility, not as undertakers in the ordinary sense but as arrangers of the dead man's standards and of the order in which his mourners should follow him. Then also, because the character of the Herald was supposed to be inviolate, they were much employed as ambassadors and bearers of important messages to foreign rulers. While these tasks are no longer entrusted to them, they have acquired a fresh function in the last 300 years and that is the keeping of pedigree records. Their main duty, however, continues to relate to coats of arms, and they have to grant arms and to regulate arms when in use.

14. When you talk of the control of arms by the College of Arms, do you mean that the use of arms by anyone and everyone in England and Wales must be controlled by the heralds?

Strictly, yes, though in practice their control is so slight as to be unexercised in very many cases. I estimate that there are in this country not less than 50,000 persons (including some corporations) who are using arms to which they are not entitled.

15. How has this situation come about?

Because the regulation of arms in England was carried out by two methods both of which became obsolete over the past 300 years. These methods were (1) Visitations or tours of inspection by the heralds. These were conducted roughly once a generation and covered one county at a time. They began in 1529 and ended in 1686. In 1688 James II abandoned his throne. His four immediate successors were not too sure of their position, and three of them were foreigners. They did not issue any commissions to their officers of arms to conduct Visitations and the practice has never been resumed. (2) The Court of Chivalry sat under the authority of the Earl Marshal, but it aroused great opposition and was abolished by the Puritans under the Commonwealth. In 1660 it was revived but did not sit after 1735 until 1954.

16. Was there not a case before the Court of Chivalry some years ago?

Yes, in 1954 the Court was impressively revived with full splendour. A test case was brought; the Manchester City

Corporation sued the Manchester Palace of Varieties because the latter used the City Arms on its drop curtain and on its documents. Judgement was given for the Manchester Corporation. Thus the existence and the jurisdiction of the Court of Chivalry was affirmed.

17. What effect has this judgement had on heraldic law breaking?

Very little. The City of London put its arms right. For some centuries the City had been using a crest and supporters without being recorded with the College of Arms, although the shield of the City arms had been duly recorded. The rectification cost £200. Generally speaking, however, the sitting of the Court of Chivalry in 1954–5 (the judgement was pronounced in 1955) has had very little effect on heraldic law breaking. Why should it? Is it likely that the Court, so laboriously convened once in two and a quarter centuries, would sit to judge the case of someone who had granted the local golf club a badge? Moreover, Lord Goddard who acted as Surrogate or Deputy to the Earl Marshal, was careful to state in his judgement that if it were the intention of the conveners to make a frequent use of the Court, they should obtain statutory authority for its pains and penalties, in other words a Bill to regularize the modern position of the Court of Chivalry. This has not been done.

18. Can anyone design his own coat of arms?

Yes, if he can square his conscience, for penalties are unlikely to be visited upon him. I recall a conversation which I had with the Garter King of Arms in 1955. I asked him if the Court would be sitting frequently or with fair frequency in the future. He replied that he did not know.

Meanwhile I recall cases such as that of a friend of mine

with whom I was standing in a pub one day. He pointed out to me a man crossing the floor whose blazer bore an heraldic device on its pocket. 'I devised that,' said my friend. 'Then you may do penance in the dungeons of Arundel Castle,' I answered. In truth there is little likelihood of the artist being summoned before the Court.

19. You have referred to the Scottish organization of heraldry. What is it?

No one ever attempted to conduct a Visitation in Scotland, though strange to say, there were three Visitations in even more unruly Ireland. Can you imagine Rob Roy MacGregor being interrogated by a herald as to the validity of his arms? To avoid tiresome difficulties of this sort, the Scots passed a law in 1672, under which the registering of arms in Scotland became obligatory within three months. Since the expiration of this period of grace, all arms borne in Scotland must be registered with the Lord Lyon in his office. If not so registered or matriculated as the term goes, the arms are illegal. The Scottish position is thus delightfully simple. Moreover, the Lord Lyon being a judge of the Court of Session, contempt of his judgements is contempt of court, punishable by fine or imprisonment. I once talked with the present Lord Lyon about ways in which the English College of Arms could cope with heraldic law breaking within its boundaries. He favoured the revival of the Visitations in England. 'I've told them,' he said, referring to the English Heralds, 'that I am prepared to come and help them, give them the benefits of my experience!' They would rather face another Bannockburn!

The plain facts are that the Scottish system works, whereas the English heraldic arrangements are better than the Scottish. A grant of arms in England lasts for ever. Anyone who can prove descent from the original grantee is entitled to use the arms. Thus although the £200 paid for a grant sounds a lot of money, it is not really so, when one realizes that it lasts for ever. Under Scottish heraldic law a grant costs only about £50, but there is the necessity of rematriculating every generation, costing some £20.

20. But I thought that one had to pay a licence each year in order to use arms?

Yes, there was once, previous to 1945, a licence of two or three guineas per year, payable for the use of arms on such articles as carriages, silver, signet rings, and others. This charge was abolished with effect from 1 January 1945, mainly because of the difficulty of collecting it. An amusing comment on governmental views of heraldry is found in the fact that the law which ordered the paying of the licences, made it clear that they must be paid without any distinction made between arms recorded with the College of Arms or self-granted and home made.

21. Can someone who possesses arms grant them to someone else?

No, the arms are granted to a particular individual and to his legitimate descendants, or to a body. However, in the case of corporations they can and frequently do give permission for their arms to be reproduced on programmes and commemoratory leaflets. Such a usage is temporary. It ought to be noted that the reproduction in a book, by way of illustration of someone's coat of arms is perfectly permissible. Not even the Duke of Norfolk can object to his coat of arms being shown in a book on heraldry or history, provided of course that the drawing is accurate.

22. Is the motto part of the coat of arms?

No. In modern grants the motto is always included but it still does not form part of the grant. You may change your motto each day if you wish. If you have inherited as your motto, *Virtus sola nobilitat,* you may change it to *What's in it for No. 1?* as being more appropriate to modern times. One word of caution. Should the motto form part of a block of your coat of arms, a new motto means a new block, and editors are reluctant to incur what will appear to them an unnecessary expense.

23. What is the queer-looking language which heraldry uses?

Ultimately it is Norman French, because during the central Middle Ages French was the language of chivalry (itself a French word) and even as late as 1348 when there occurred the pestilence known as the Black Death, French was still the language of the Court and the monarchy. Half a century later English had taken its place, though it was an English which had itself been much influenced by the Norman French of 300 years past. About 1400 there was a movement in England to use English terms in place of foreign ones, as 'gold' for 'or' etc., but this did not succeed.

In fact it is not hard to learn heraldic language. The essential terms can be learned in a week; as to the rest they are very numerous and it is not worth while to burden your memory with them. Some of them occur perhaps half a dozen times at most in the life of an heraldic student. How much less frequently then in the life of the ordinary reader. 'Yale', for instance, is the name of a mythical monster which was one of the Queen's Beasts set up outside Westminster Abbey at the time of the Coronation, but the term is otherwise very rarely used.

24. What are the various parts of the coat of arms?

The shield, in the centre. On top of it should come a helmet, and on top of that a crest which is supposed to be bound on to the helmet by a wreath of the colours. This is

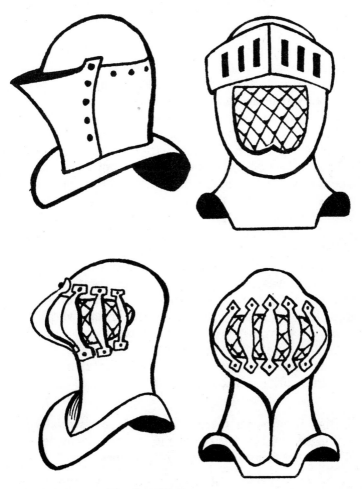

Fig. 1 – HELMS
(showing rank)

Upper left: Esquire or Gentleman.   Lower left. Peer.
Upper right: Knight or Baronet.   Lower right. Sovereign.

shown in six partitions, one and one, being the two principal colours of the shield. From the helmet flow down the lambrequin or mantlet which, like everything else in heraldry had a strictly utilitarian function. Made originally of linen or cloth, the lambrequin helped to keep off the heat of the sun and also catch or deflect sword cuts. Over the main body armour was worn the surcoat.

Some persons are allowed figures on either side of their shields. These are called supporters. They are the prerogative of peers, Knights of the Garter, of the Thistle and of St. Patrick and of Knights Grand Cross of the other British Orders of Chivalry. In Scotland things are arranged differently, and in addition to the owners of supporters just listed, many of the untitled lairds are allowed supporters.

Again, in the case of a Knight of the Garter, he may have his shield surrounded by the ribbon of the Garter. Other knighthoods may be signalized in this way, and so may membership (without title) in the lesser orders. A man who has the C.V.O., O.B.E., etc., may hang them from his shield rather like inn signs. Finally, the shield and whole coat of arms may be represented on a compartment which hovers rather like Swift's Flying Island of Laputa. Still it is an improvement upon the old-fashioned Victorian gas bracket as groundwork for a coat of arms.

25. Does it not seem strange that all these essentially practical things should have survived and now be used by people who will never put on armour unless it be in fancy dress?

Yes, but heraldry managed to survive the disuse of armour, because it had become (*a*) ornamental and (*b*) a symbol of gentility. With the latter its fortune was made, for if arms were the sign of gentle blood, then no one was going to forgo them merely because their wording and symbolism was centuries out of date. Even England's greatest poet was not above armorial ambitions and pursued a coat of arms until he obtained it, and the right to have the description 'gentleman' on his burial register.

26. What is the meaning of the term esquire?

Although this is more properly dealt with in our last section we can consider it here, for anyone who obtains a grant of arms is automatically created an esquire, since this term occurs in the grant. As late as about 1870, Queen Victoria created her favourite servant, John Brown an esquire, without any question of arms. Originally an esquire was the follower of a knight, one who himself aspired to wear the gilded spurs. Gradually the term came to be applied to persons who were of gentle birth and who were of the class from which the knights were made. In course of time elaborate rules were framed to define the classes of persons who could be termed esquire. These rules still exist but have become almost obsolete owing to the well-nigh universal popular use of esquire on commercial communications.

27 What are the objects called which appear on a shield?

Legion would be a not unfair answer. First comes the groundwork of the shield. This must be a colour, a metal or a fur. Then on top of this ground come the charges as they are called. These fall into two classes, the honourable ordinaries, and the extraordinary charges. The former are charges or marks which are very common, such as the cross, or the bend or chief. As to the extraordinary, there is hardly any limit to them. Almost anything can have an heraldic significance.

28. What are the heraldic colours?

There are five principal colours which are here given with

their heraldic name, and in parenthesis, the English translation of them. Azure (blue), gules (red), purpure (purple), sable (black) and vert (green). There are also two less common heraldic colours, namely tenné (tawney) and sanguine (murrey).

29. What are the metals?

There are two, these being or (gold) and argent (silver).

30. What are the furs?

There are seven. These are (1) ermine (white with black spots) and two variants of ermine, (2) ermines (black with white spots), (3) erminois (gold with black spots). Ermine was the luxury fur of the Middle Ages, hence no doubt its use. Then come (4) pean (black with gold spots); and (5) vair. This last was originally of pieces of fur but is now shown as silver and blue and arranged in rows opposed to each other. There are also (6) counter vair, which is a variety of (5); and (7) potent counterpoint, in which the silver and blue are alternate, the blue portions taking the form of inverted Ts.

31. How are the colours, metals and furs used?

As the ground of the shield. The heraldic rule is that a colour must not be used upon a colour, a metal upon a metal or a fur upon a fur. There are, however, so many exceptions to this rule that it must I think, have been of late origin.

32. What is the significance of the charges in heraldry?

With this question we come nearest to the realm of myth. All sorts of stories are current about the meaning of this,

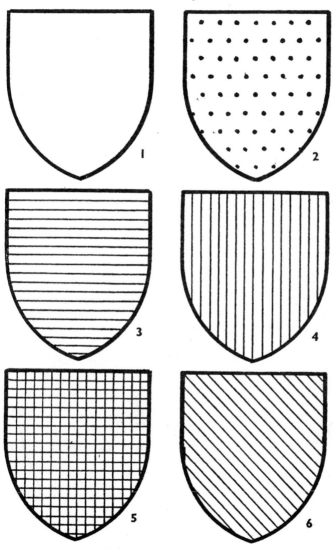

Fig. 2 – PETRA SANCTA
(Hatching to indicate tinctures)

Metals:
1 Argent (Silver)   3 Azure (Blue)   5 Sable (Black)
2 Or (Gold)   4 Gules (Red)   6 Vert (Green)

that and the other in a coat of arms. Most of these stories can be discounted. The origin of arms which are at all old must in the majority of cases be lost in impenetrable darkness. As to modern arms, i.e. those granted in the last three or four centuries, in many cases their meaning can be discovered by research. Often the charge is a play on a name, a spear for Shakespeare, a fish weir for Wear, etc., in many other instances there is a reference to some circumstance in the life of the grantee. With the oldest arms, such as azure a bend or (blue with a gold bend) the coat may originally have been simply an easy design in someone's favourite colours.

33. How old is heraldry (or as a questioner put it to me at a recent lecture) – who invented heraldry?

Heraldry in western Europe appeared about the middle of the twelfth century (see answer to question 1). As to the inventor of it, we are completely in the dark as to whether it was in fact invented by one man or was a general movement, born of the need for distinguishing signs in battle. Owing to the fact that newsapers were not invented until some 300 years ago, we are often ignorant as to the time or manner of appearance of various changes. We can say of heraldry that it was not in existence before the Norman Conquest of England in 1066. The shields of the warriors on the Bayeux Tapestry do not show heraldic designs. When we move on a generation to the time of the First Crusade, 1095–9, we find a good account of the western knights in the writings of a learned lady, Anna Comnena, daughter of the Greek Emperor. She says nothing of any designs on the shields of the knights, though her description of their appearance and armour is exact. The first evidence we have of a coat of arms appears on an enamel of 1127 which shows Henry I of England arming his son-in-law, the Count of Anjou. Thereafter the evidences multiply rapidly, and during the rest of the twelfth century we have plenty of seals, and other monuments which show coats of arms.

We have only to reflect upon the history of the aeroplane in the last sixty or so years, and the large part which its story has taken in the newspapers, to realize that a modern innovation is at once chronicled in the Press; lacking this powerful aid in the Middle Ages we cannot do more than surmise as to the origin and growth of heraldry.

34. I would like more detail as to the cessation of the Visitations to which you refer in the answer to question 15

Yes, the position about the Visitations is that they were regularly conducted from 1529 (when Henry VIII issued the first commission to the heralds) until 1686. They were part of the movement, general in Europe, for the Crown in each country to control all matters of honours and titles; in England this movement obtained keener edge from the Tudor desire to control everything in the country after the near anarchy of the Wars of the Roses. So the sovereigns began to issue commissions to the officials of their College of Arms to visit one county at a time. The practice would be to go down to, e.g. Berkshire, and stay at the house of the principal nobleman, and thence to issue a proclamation requiring everyone to come in and register his arms. The heralds had the power to make the person disclaim his arms, that is declare that they were not his. Such disclaimers were often posted in the offender's home town, in the market-place, which must have been a frightful blow to the well-known English trait of snobbery and of 'keeping up with the Joneses'. However, many lists of such disclaimers exist, and in some cases the reasons are given. A man's only evidence for the use of arms by his family was an old red seal of his grandfather's. This was not considered sufficient, to justify the use of arms. Sometimes the arms were respited, as it was termed, for further proof. In one case of a family still current in the pedigree books, this respiting has lasted since the end of the Visitation period, so that for more than 250 years proof has been awaited. In another instance, the heralds when they visited one of the Midland shires, undertook to write up the pedigree of the nobleman with whom they had been staying. The notes they made were left behind at the country seat, and have never been written up, though 350 years have passed.

35. Do cases ever occur in which a grant of arms is made to a man, and then later it is discovered that his ancestors had lawful arms? If so, what happens in such cases?

Yes, cases of this can and do occur. I know of one instance in which a man who had become the High Sheriff of a county, and had as such to have a banner with his arms displayed, obtained a grant of arms, somewhat in a hurry. I should explain that if an inquiry is made of the College of Arms to find out if someone had arms, it can easily occur that the grant of arms some generations back could be overlooked, because the pedigree of the ensuing generations had not been recorded there, and so the connection with the grantee is not clear. This must have happened in the case cited, for the arms grant went through in order for the grantee to have arms to use on his banner; but later his son made further investigations into the matter and found that there had been an arms grant some generations earlier. Now the family use only the coat of arms of the earlier vintage. The more modern coat is retained and shown to the curious, only as a curiosity. In fact, the modern family have the right to use both coats of arms. This sort of anomaly used to occur more frequently in the past than at present, and it is the origin of the, at first sight, puzzling practice which one finds in accounts of eighteenth- and early nineteenth-century coats of arms, in which two coats of arms of the same family name are quartered together. Thus: 1 and 4 Smith

Ancient; 2 and 3 Smith Modern. It only means that there have been two coats of arms granted or registered for the same family. This habit of using both arms in the same coat does not now prevail.

36. What do you mean by quartering?

Quartering is the showing of four coats of arms in the same shield. The best-known example is that of the royal family arms, in which we have the shield divided into four quarters. In the top right hand (a shield must always be thought of as held by someone and therefore the left of the shield as it faces us, is really the right hand of it), appear the arms of England. Then these will appear again in the bottom left, which is No. 4. In the top left No. 2 come the arms of Scotland, and in the bottom right No. 3 are the arms of Ireland. This usage of quartering different shields is used to denote, as in the royal arms, the union of the crowns, and of the national arms. It is also used to denote family alliances. Perhaps we had better come to this part of the explanation through the answer to another but allied question.

37. How are the arms of husband and wife shown?

In heraldry the man is supreme, unless he happens, as in rare cases, to marry a queen who is sovereign in her own right. So if a woman comes from a family which has arms (i.e. is armigerous) and her husband does not possess arms, then her arms cannot be shown. There is no shield on which to display them. A very uncomfortable position, for the husband that is, and one which has led many a man to petition the College of Arms for a grant. But if the husband has been sensible, and has arms, then the normal practice is to divide his shield by a straight line down the middle, put his coat of arms on the right and those of his wife's family on the left. This method is known as impaling, or dimidiating (i.e. halving). Now, should the wife be what is known as an heraldic heiress (quite different by the way from being an heiress in the financial sense) then a different practice prevails. The man's arms fill the shield but with a small shield put on the middle of his shield. This small shield is called an escutcheon of pretence.

38. Can the children of a marriage where both parents are armigerous use the arms of both father and mother?

Only when the mother was an heiress or co-heiress as described above. In that case the children of the marriage can quarter the arms of mother and father. In other words, their shield is divided into four equal parts and the father's arms occur in 1 and 4, while those of the mother come in 2 and 3. It can easily be imagined how confusing the set up can be when, with the passage of a few generations, and marriages to heiresses in each generation, the shield gets cluttered up with quarterings. Resort has to be had to the practice known as grandquartering, and that I leave to the reader's imagination. There are instances of noble families, whose quarterings run into the hundred. One case had over 300 quarterings, while in the families of such great noblemen as the Duke of Atholl there are supposed to be as many as a thousand quarterings. To do justice to such an array, one would need a very large hall or castle window.

If the mother was not an heiress, then no suggestion of quartering arises, and the children of two armigerous parents can use only their father's coat of arms.

39. You referred to the arms of a prince consort? How are they shown?

Generally by shirking the issue. I have never seen a representation of the arms of Prince Philip in the same shield with those of the Queen. If they were to be shown together, then I would think that the arms of the Prince should appear on the left of the shield with those of the Queen on the right, just as though the Queen were the husband. The reason for this inversion of the normal arrangement is that the Queen though Philip's wife is also his sovereign, since sex does not enter into the conception of the monarchy in England. The sovereign of England is sovereign irrespective of sex. Moreover, the royal arms of England are those of the country, since they have been used by every dynasty – Tudor, Stuart, Hanoverian and Windsor – since they were first adopted by the Plantaganets, Richard I being the first sovereign to employ a recognized coat of arms.

If we look back to the last Prince Consort, then we find a recognition of the principle which I have set out above, albeit in a very peculiar form. For the arms of Prince Albert of Saxe-Coburg and Gotha, the husband of Queen Victoria, and the great-great-grandfather of both the Queen and Prince Philip, were represented with those of England, but in a quarterly form as though he had been Queen Victoria's son instead of her husband. This form did, however, show that the Prince was a subject of the Queen, like all other of her subjects, although he was her husband also.

In the Middle Ages, we sometimes find the example of a man of lower rank than his wife who has his arms on the left of the shield while hers are on the right. In some cases, too, a man of low degree will bear his wife's arms alone.

40. What about a woman who is not married, and who has arms, can she show them on a shield?

On a shield, no, unless she is a sovereign in her own right, like the Virgin Queen, Elizabeth I. A single woman can bear arms on a lozenge or diamond shaped compartment, and without a crest. Despite the occurrence occasionally in the Middle Ages of someone like Joan of Arc, it was the general view that ladies did not take part in war, and so could not have either shield or crest. The bearing of arms on a lozenge is the rule for a woman who is a maiden lady, or again for a widow, or a divorcee who has not remarried.

41. What is the position of heraldry today? Are many coats of arms granted?

Yes, many grants of arms are made each year, and these to private individuals. Indeed, I should be inclined to think that heraldry has never been more widespread or had a greater interest for so many people. Most of the officers of the College of Arms or of the Lyon Office are very busy, and much occupied. Not only do private individuals take out grants of arms, but many corporate bodies do so. Since the war there have been many grants of arms which take in the nationalized industries, some large modern corporations, such as the Atomic Energy Authority, and many cases of arms for countries which have been carved out of the old British Empire. Again, there have been many grants of arms to the big banks, insurance companies, and to other businesses. I found quite recently that of the five big banks ('the Big Five'), only one had had an arms grant as far back as 1928; of the others, one had had a grant in the 1930s and the remaining three since the last war. Then again, we must remember that many coats of arms have been taken out by people who before the war would have been very unlikely to have applied for arms. Now that the Labour Party has become so to speak acclimatized in England, the Labour peers have taken out arms, and many other comparatively 'new' folk have done the same. Then too there is the supply of arms to Americans.

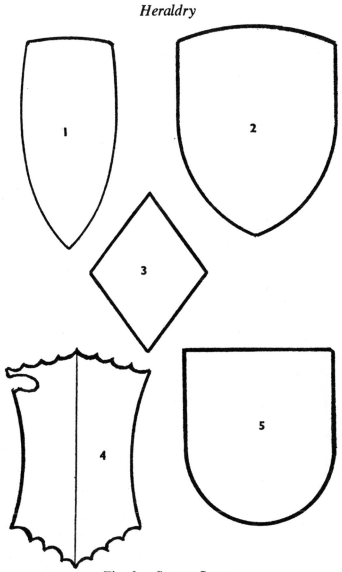

Fig. 3 – SHIELD SHAPES
1. Flat-iron (Norman) 13th Century
2 Modified form 14th Century onwards
3 Lozenge used by ladies
4 Florid form (series of concave curves) late 14th Century. Also showing 'Bouche' for resting lance.
5 Continental form of Shield with semicircular Base.

42. Do Americans care at all for heraldry?

It would be easy on the evidence of my own postbag to say that a great many do, but one must remember the vast population of the States. However, I think it fair to say that a large number of Americans are keen on titles and heraldry. Many of them come over or write to England, in order to obtain a grant of arms. Others who are of Scottish descent go to the Lyon Office. At one time so busy were the heralds in satisfying their transatlantic clients that a cartoon in one of the papers showed the tabarded figures getting the pedigrees down the assembly line for shipment to America. It was about this time (a few years after the war) that an American approached me and asked me to get him a coat of arms. I set out to do so, and almost before I had begun my work in contacting the College of Arms, the officer who was to deal with his case was astonished to receive sterling to the value of £105 (then the charge for a grant), from the American gentleman. For the next eleven months while his grant was being prepared, I received numerous letters asking me for 'the bearings'.

There are, however, more Americans who do not feel that they should approach the sovereign of a foreign state for a grant of arms. Or else they do not know enough about the matter to do so. At any rate, some scholarly Americans long ago formed themselves into a body which registers, and in some cases actually grants, arms. This is the Committee on Heraldry of the New England Historic Genealogical Society. It issues Rolls of Arms, an old English practice extinct in this country for some centuries. These Rolls of Arms are entirely authentic and worth while. It would be a good thing if more Americans had their names put on to them. I understand that a similar body exists in the southern states of the Union.

To these two classes in which authentic heraldry is flourishing, we have to add a much larger section of the armigerous Americans, and that is composed of people whose thirst for gentility must be slaked at lower costs. An American correspondent of mine told me of a lady in the U.S.A. who showed him an illustration of her coat of arms. He asked where she got it, and she replied, 'From an old man who called at the door.' She added that 'he was a rather dirty old man'. I have myself seen advertisements of 'grants' of arms for so many dollars, pictures for more, and pedigrees for even larger sums. These initial charges may run for as little as five to ten dollars. The persons who run these businesses are well informed, for my correspondent went on to say that he had challenged them as to why they were using his (duly registered) coat of arms. He got the reply that they did not use his coat but the coat of the family in general to which he belonged. There is some shadow of justification for this reply. It need not be added, that despite such a principle, many American families are receiving arms to which they are not entitled. Their surnames are the same as those of armigerous English and Scottish families, but beyond that they have nothing to commend them to the bearing of these so-called ancestral arms.

43. What about heraldry in other parts of the world, outside the British Isles and the U.S.A.?

There is a considerable volume of heraldry; in countries such as Canada, Australia and New Zealand, it is largely controlled from England and Scotland. In South Africa, something of the same sort applies, but there recently an Act was passed for the setting up of a heraldic establishment, which would grant arms and register pedigrees as well as regulate the state ceremonies. In continental Europe, heraldry has had a chequered and often unhappy history in the present century. One of the great forces in maintaining heraldry is a monarchy, and so many of the great monarchies of the past have been driven out of their countries that the practice of heraldry has been difficult. When there is a monarchy, the sovereign will always want to control the heraldry of the country because coats of arms are just as much honours as titles are, and therefore must be controlled by the sovereign as he or she is the Fountain (or source) of Honour. Consequently when a monarchy is abolished, the means of controlling heraldry goes too. This is the case with Germany, Austria, Russia, and now Italy. France has no heraldic system of value. Spain owing to its adherence to the past, is better in heraldry and extensive studies of the subject come out each year. Portugal, too, has not neglected its heraldic wealth. It can be imagined what havoc the Communist régimes in eastern Europe have made of heraldry. Outside the countries mentioned, there are relics of heraldry in the Philippines, in India, in some other countries of Asia. In Japan there is an age-old system of the use of crests which is very close to the Western style. In fact Japan is the only country in the world outside the area of western Europe, in which we can be sure that an heraldic system has developed.

44. What are difference marks?

They are used to distinguish the different degrees of cadency in a family. These degrees arise from the position of the various sons. Thus the eldest son (in the lifetime of his father) bore on his shield a label; the second son bore a crescent; the third a mullet and the fourth a martlet (i.e. bird without feet, the fourth son being likely to have no land to alight on, as with John Lackland!) and so on. The use of these cadency marks has gone very much out of fashion in England, where one can see all sorts of cadets of a family using the full arms which are applicable only to the head. The royal family do use cadency marks, and these are labels which bear on them the distinguishing designs

Fig. 4 – CADENCY MARKS

(Indicating various sons on paternal arms).

1 Label	5 Annulet
2 Crescent	6 Fleur-de-lys
3 Mullet	7 Rose
4 Martlet	8 Cross Moline
9 Octofoil, or double quatrefoil	

approved by the sovereign. It is not always realized that the members of the royal, unlike other families, have no right to arms as such, but must await the pleasure of the sovereign. Thus, when a son of the sovereign is created a duke, he will receive a grant of the royal arms suitably differenced, and this will mean that a label is shown over the top of the arms with certain marks upon it, such as a crown, or a lion, or an anchor. In Scottish heraldry, however, the use of difference marks is imperative, owing to the system of matriculation, which requires special marks for each generation, as they matriculate their arms.

45. What are hatchments?

They are the display of arms over the door of a house when a person who was armigerous has died. The practice was once very common in England, and anyone who visits old country churches is likely to see several specimens of hatchments hanging in the church or the vestry. Very rarely is a hatchment used today, but a few years ago one was displayed at the death of Lady Catherine Ashburnham, the last of a very ancient family. The hatchment follows the rule of arms, by showing the arms of a man on a shield, or those of a lady, if single, on a lozenge.

46. What are the Seize Quartiers?

Here again is the sort of heraldic stuff which delights the historical novelist, or even the serious historian. To talk of sixteen quarterings is always somewhat dangerous. The term denotes the continental idea of tracing a man's ancestry through both sides, and showing that each family in turn was armigerous. The seize quartiers are the sixteen ancestors from whom a man descends. To render them complete, the table must show that each of the sixteen ancestors was armigerous. The idea is to get back to eight great-great-grandparents all of whom were entitled to arms. Sir Bernard Burke, who evidently did not like the idea, said 'according to our English notions, this test is rather, I think, one of curiosity than real value; for compare the continental nobility, which very generally still possess it, with our nobility, which very rarely does, and observe the difference between them. Our own aristocracy yields to none other in high breeding, honour, and brilliancy of ancestry; and yet, comparatively speaking, few even among that elevated class can trace their descent up to sixteen families on both sides entitled to armorial bearings.' To which I would add that the preoccupation of continental nobility with marrying only into their own class, has given them an exclusiveness which the English nobility has never possessed; but it is also very much responsible for the overthrow of the continental nobility, because they were viewed as a class apart from the mass of the people. The English nobility, however, are closely allied with every class, and so too is our royalty, this giving a stability to our institutions which the continent has lacked. (See answer to question 6, for royal connections with the bulk of the nation.)

47. What are the best books on heraldry for reading and instruction?

I shall include this question only because I am so frequently asked it. It would be invidious to do more than to mention my own books on the subject. I shall merely remark of them, that *Teach Yourself Heraldry*, is designed to help the student who knows nothing of heraldry and to lead him on to a fair knowledge of the subject; and that *The Story of Heraldry* is a more advanced book, which requires some heraldic knowledge to appreciate.

Coming to books by other authors, I should strongly recommend those by the late A. C. Fox-Davies. *Heraldry Explained* is out of print. It is a small work, and very useful in giving clear expositions of the subject. Copies can be obtained secondhand. Then there is the author's larger work, *Complete Guide to Heraldry*, which is in print, and which has been brought up to date. This is a very fine book, partly for reading, partly for browsing. The author produced other works on heraldry, including his *Armorial Families*, and his *Book of Public Arms*. All of them are well worth getting for reference. His main defect was his dogmatism as to the past of heraldry, for the rules governing modern heraldry were by Fox-Davies applied to the past where they did not always by any means apply.

The writings of Sir Bernard Burke abound in heraldry and in references to the same. His main work in this respect is his *General Armory*, without which no student of heraldry can hope to deal with the innumerable references which he will encounter. This work has been produced afresh in recent years and can be obtained for seven guineas. When it was out of print, it sometimes fetched as much as £28. It gives the reference to almost every coat of arms known in the British Isles up to the time when the text was last revised, in 1884. In addition it has a very useful glossary of heraldic terms, plus an introduction and notes.

2

Ancestors

48. What are ancestors?

The dictionary answer is, one from whom one has descended, a forefather. The word is derived from the French, *ancêstre*, itself coming from *antecessor*, Latin from *antecedere*, to go before. It may seem a very simple question to ask and answer, but if we say that Queen Elizabeth II is the descendant of Queen Elizabeth I, or to put it another way round, that Queen Elizabeth I was the ancestress of the present Queen, we shall at once be answered with an indignant exclamation: 'But Queen Elizabeth I didn't marry!' So at the very beginning we have to explain the difference between direct ancestry and collateral. The term 'direct ancestor' is rather misleading. There cannot be an indirect ancestor in the proper sense of the word. By 'direct ancestor' we must always mean someone from whom one has descended. The indirect ancestor is the collateral. While it is untrue that Her present Majesty has descended directly from the Tudor Queen Elizabeth, she is certainly a kinswoman of hers, since Queen Elizabeth of Tudor days was a niece of Queen Margaret of Scotland, the daughter of Henry VII, who married James IV of Scotland. Without going into these exalted and distant relationships, you need only think of some of your uncles and aunts, who are obviously connected with you by blood, but from whom you do not descend.

49. Why trace your ancestry?

A very pertinent question and one which many people would have been wise to ask themselves, as we shall see in the course of our questions and answers. The brief reply is – to find out where we came from. That should always be the right answer, and in the majority of cases of ancestry tracing it is the right one, but there are many examples of people who have embarked on pedigree research for unworthy motives, such as bolstering up their own vanity, and running after titles which they can never obtain, and which would be a great expense to them if they could get them. However, the aim to discover one's forebears and to find out as much as possible about them is as legitimate as most forms of human curiosity.

50. What is a pedigree?

A genealogical table, i.e. a drawn out account of how someone is descended. The word is said to come from the French *pied de grue* or crane's foot, taken from the marks used in showing descent on a pedigree table. Pedigrees or genealogical tables abound in the general run of history books, for one cannot properly understand such historical periods as the Wars of the Roses, or the War of the Spanish Succession, or the conflicting claims of the Stuarts and Hanoverians, unless a table is provided to show the relationship of the various cousins who had anything but cousinly love for each other.

51. Are pedigrees only for the 'nobs'?

No, they are the right way to set out anyone's line of descent. If you can show only your descent from your grandfather, then you ought to have a pedigree because without one it will not be easy to know the degrees of relationship of your cousins, uncles, aunts, etc. Many people think of pedigree as something which belongs only to very exalted folk, dukes, marquesses and the like. Well, it may come as a surprise to many such people to learn that in many so-called humble pedigrees, there are numerous cases of distinguished names turning up. A few years ago when Prince Andrew was born, a table was published to show his descent on father's and mother's side. On his mother's side, that of the Queen, there were plenty of plain misters, because the Queen Mother's forebears had intermarried with people who were not of grand family and who were untitled. This is a very common phenomenon in the pedigrees of a vast number of British people. The reason is very simple. In continental Europe the royal family circles kept very much to themselves, and formed a kind of marriage trade union. The same thing happened with the nobility, so that they were not contaminated with commoner folk. In England and Scotland, however, these rules were not observed, so that from royalty to peasant, there were degrees of relationship over several generations. The consequence is that many distinguished connections turn up in families of plain folk, who are very often quite surprised at their noble and even royal affiliations.

52. How far can you go back with a pedigree in this country?

Provided that, as far as you know, your family has lived in England for some centuries – and not come here from Europe within the last few decades – then with any reasonable luck you should be able to get back 200, 250 or 300 years. There is nothing unusual in a pedigree of tradesmen or yokels going back some 300 years. I have known many such, and they witness to a stability in British institutions which many Continental countries would envy. For stability means that records have a much better chance of being kept than where there is trouble, and civil commotion.

53. How do you do it?

This is really the biggest question of all in this subject and I think that before I answer it, I ought to consider another question I am often asked, namely – Are there people who will undertake research for one? Yes, and their charges vary enormously. I knew one research worker who never undertook a case at a fee less than 100 guineas. There are many cheaper labourers in the genealogical field, and they may begin your research at charges as low as five guineas though I doubt whether with all-round price increases anyone now would begin at less than ten guineas. If you do go to one of these workers, you will find that charges must increase with time and the work done, so that if one begins at, say, ten guineas, there will have to be further charges as one progresses. The essential thing to grasp, if you employ someone else to do your research is that you must pay for that person's time. Suppose that they search a parish register for two or three days, even without any successful result as far as your ancestry is concerned, they must still support themselves during that time. Therefore if you are employing them for the work, you must pay for their time. If on the other hand you do it yourself then, you are providing the time.

54. What then is the cost, if I do it myself?

There are various do-it-yourself kits, so to speak, and quite a large number of books exist which profess to give you information on the subject. Among these, perhaps I may mention modestly, are some of my own, but there are others, and most libraries will find you a book on the subject of tracing your ancestry. In addition, as I will show in process of question and answer there are many reference works which are useful to you in tracing your family history. For the cost, apart from the charges of an employed genealogist, the amount involved in obtaining certificates and official documents is small. Very rarely does the charge exceed £1, unless some will has to be copied, or some document at the Public Record Office translated from medieval script. Even then the official scale of charges is very moderate and reasonable.

55. Well then, where do I start and how do I set about it?

You begin with yourself, which is quite natural and right. You start off with your own birth certificate. Then you must determine whether you want to trace father's or mother's side. In other words you have to be either a normal person or a feminist. Perhaps it is not quite as bad as that alternative sounds. Seriously if you try to trace both sides of your family you will end in about two or three years with a pedigree of a truly formidable width but of very little depth, for each generation doubles, so that while we have two parents, we have four grandparents and so on. Tracing these is quite a task. I advise, then, that you decide to trace one parent's line, and not both. Choosing then, you must next have the marriage certificate of your parents. You know how old they are or were, but could you state exactly the date of their birth? The day of the month no doubt, but what about the year. I have known some of my hearers answer up without a falter, 1873, or whatever it happened to be, but answers such as, 'well he was in the first war, but he wasn't in the first batch, so I think he must have been out of the late teens in 1914' or that sort of thing will not do. Believe me, you would be surprised at the number of well-equipped folk whose answers as to parents' years of birth take some such form.

56. Where do I go for these certificates?

To Somerset House, in the Strand, London. There are a great many valuable documents here, apart from birth, marriage and death certificates, including much interesting material about the income tax affairs of thousands of citizens. However, for the moment we are concerned with Somerset House as the repository of certificates of birth, marriage and death. Owing to the activities of the Welfare State and the thirst for personal information which it has caused, many people now go into the galleries of Somerset House who would never have been seen there in days gone by. I cannot help recalling a conversation which I involuntarily overheard as I was leaving there one day. Two women had been inside the building to obtain the marriage certificate of one of them. Result, a negative search. The dialogue which followed was most amusing. It consisted of downright scepticism on the part of the one woman, and on the other side, a catalogue of dates, which were remembered chiefly because of the second woman's association at some time with various men. On another occasion, a man whose birth was not legitimate spent over two hours searching the books for his birth certificate. He then got someone better skilled than himself to visit the records, and they produced the necessary information very quickly, by the simple expedient of looking for his birth under his mother's and not under his (putative) father's name. Lastly, there can sometimes be seen in the Strand a sandwich-board man with a large notice, somewhat hard to decipher but the purport of which is that he has been deprived of his pension because the details of birth cannot be found at Somerset House.

All of which may serve to warn you that when you arrive there, you should seek the help of the courteous officials whose duty it is to assist you. In addition to much useful verbal assistance they will get you some leaflets which will explain much to you, as to how to look for the certificates. Charges amount to a few shillings, and the certificates will arrive within a day or two.

At Somerset House you cannot go back beyond 1837 when the registration of births, marriages and deaths began in England and Wales. Scotland was later, in 1855, and Ireland not until 1864. There are gaps in the records, a few here and there when someone's birth was not entered. This accounts for the difficulties met by some people who are trying to get a pension.

57. You say that Somerset House goes back to 1837, but what about the time before that?

In theory for 300 years before Somerset House recording began, the vital statistics on birth, marriage and death, were kept in the records of each parish. I say, in theory, because although the parish records are supposed to begin in 1538, in fact they do not start at that date in a great many cases. The celebrated historian of the parish registers, the late Mr. A. M. Burke, says that failure to comply with the order to keep the records was of constant occurrence. This was not unnatural for the order emanated from Thomas Cromwell, Henry VIII's tyrannical Vicar-General, and all sorts of sinister motives were attributed to him in making this order. It was even suggested that he had a mind to put taxes on births, marriages and deaths. However, as a budding genealogist you are concerned with the record of your ancestors. In practice most parish records begin in the seventeenth century, and you should find this a great help to you in tracing your ancestry before 1837.

58. This is all very well, but how am I to get from the state registers of 1837 on to the parish registers?

There are about 14,000 parishes in the Church of England in England and Wales, and if the last parish mentioned on a certificate at Somerset House does not give you the parish of your ancestor, then all you have got to do is to run through the remaining 13,999. This is facetious, but it is a serious problem or would be if we had not some fortunate help in the matter. Generally speaking anyone living today would be able to get back to the marriage of his or her great-grandparents through the records at Somerset House. In my case to take one instance, I am able to reach the marriage date of my great-grandparents at Somerset House about 1850. Fortunately a bridge does exist over which you can travel from these records to get into the parish records. This is the census return for 1851.

59. How can the census return help me?

Very much indeed. The first census return which was kept was that of 1841, and this also can be looked up at the Public Record Office in Chancery Lane (it was originally a home for converted Jews), but although it is often very useful it does not give the place of birth of the entrant. When the idea of a census was first broached in England, there was a great deal of opposition to the suggestion on the supposition that it would bring down divine vengeance upon England. However, with the progress of events, including the loss of the American colonies, the French Revolution, and the rise of Napoleon, the people felt no doubt that they could risk a little more, and so in 1801, ten years after the Americans had decided to hold a census, one was held in Britain. For the first time it was known how many people lived in the island, total some 12 millions. But once the return had been made, the detailed papers were destroyed. It took some genius in the civil service to suggest that it might be worth while to keep the papers, and that was not until 1841. Even then, from a genealogical point of view, the records are not all that they should be. When it came to asking the entrant his place of birth, the recorders could only think of saying, 'were you born in this parish?' i.e. the place where the entrant was living at that time. It took another ten years and another genius – someone of the same calibre as the man who first thought of using fire – to substitute the master inquiry, 'Where were you born?' This first appeared in 1851. If you take the place where your great-grandfather lived in or about 1850–2 – and as I have explained you can get this as a rule from the records at Somerset House – then you can look up the particular parish in the 1851 census returns (this costs less than 2*s*.). Very often you will find that he lived at the same place as that mentioned on his marriage or other certificate. If not, you will at least have the answer, and that turns you on to the local parish where you can look up the parish records or get the clergyman to do it for you. If you want to find his name look in the details listed in Crockford's *Clerical Directory of the Church of England*, where all C. of E. clergymen are listed.

60. What if my ancestors were Nonconformists?

Here you may get some help because at Somerset House there are preserved records older than those of 1837 and which relate to the statistics of the Nonconformist bodies.

61. What about parishes in Scotland and in Ireland?

In Scotland, parish registers unlike those in England are gathered under one roof. They do not usually go back to the same date as their English counterparts, but being all together, they are much easier to search. Conversely, this togetherness could result in a sad loss if some catastrophe were to descend upon H.M. Register House, Edinburgh. This is what happened in Ireland, where in 1922 (please note after the wicked British had left), the commotions among the Irish led to the destruction of the Four Courts and to large quantities of Irish family history records. It is very unusual to find parish records available in Ireland, but to make up for this Irish genealogists have laboured hard to find other sources of information.

62. What of Quaker or Roman Catholic records, i.e. of bodies separated from the established churches in England or Scotland?

The Quakers have been very careful in keeping their records, both in England and in America, and I would suggest that you should contact the Secretary of the Religious Society of Friends, Friends House, Euston Road, London, N.W.1. Roman Catholic records can be found through the Catholic Record Society, St. Edward's, Sutton Park, Guildford, Surrey.

63. What about the Huguenots?

This is a very important subject, because a lot of people whose names are undoubtedly French are under the impression that they are of Norman descent, whereas in reality they come from the Huguenot influx in the seventeenth century. For particulars of this source apply to the Hon. Sec., The Huguenot Society, c/o Barclays Bank, 1 Pall Mall East, London, S.W.1., or the same source but c/o The Society of Genealogists, 37 Harrington Gardens, Kensington, London, S.W.7.

64. What other public sources are there?

An immense number, indeed it is hard to say where they begin and end. However, I expect you mean that there are some special sources in London, which are of more than ordinary value. Yes, there are the Public Record Office, which I have mentioned in my answer to question 59, and which holds a huge quantity of valuable documents; the British Museum Library, in Bloomsbury, where every printed book in the history of publishing in England is available; and the Society of Genealogists at 37 Harrington Gardens, Kensington, S.W.7. I should say that you would be well advised to consult these, but not to do so until you have a very firm grasp of the principles of ancestor research, although it is true that at the Society of Genealogists you would find a number of useful text books, and also the whole library there is arranged in such a way as to help the researcher, and to save him time. For wills, you must consult the Principal Probate Registry at Somerset House, where all wills have been stored since the passing of the Probate Act in 1858.

65. What about wills before that date?

Before 1858 wills were under the jurisdiction of the Church as they had been from the beginning in England, and they were dealt with in various ecclesiastical courts over the length and breadth of the country. If, however, a man happened to have property in more than one area, in more than one ecclesiastical jurisdiction, then the will could not be handled locally but had to go to the Prerogative Court of Canterbury, known as P.C.C. to researchers. These P.C.C. wills have been lodged at Somerset House. For the other wills which did not go to P.C.C., they are situated in many places in the country, and the best course is to consult a book especially devoted to them, namely *Wills and Their Whereabouts*, by A. J. Camp.

66. You said that most English or Scots or Welsh folk could go back some 200–300 years. What about tracing ancestry before that time?

It depends very much upon what social class your ancestors belonged to. If they were landed folk, in some way owners of land or even tenants, then there would probably have been a record of them. If they were substantial tradesmen or functionaries in a town, again there would be record. If they did not belong to these two classes, there would not be the same likelihood of finding out anything about them. This applies equally in England or Scotland, and even more in Ireland. In England some classes of the community who were not very exalted can be traced for some generations, notably in the case of the villeins, who were normally bought and sold with the land. As it was of great importance to them to establish their freedom, they used to struggle hard to show that their fathers or grand-fathers had been free. Hence sometimes four or five genera-tions of villein pedigree. But as a rule, unless your family belonged to the better classes you are not likely to trace it before 1500. As for the number of pedigrees which can be traced in the Middle Ages, these are much fewer than those after 1500 or 1600. They are the pedigrees of the county families as they used to be called in England, of the lairds in Scotland. Many of them have had to sell up their landed property in recent years owing to the pressure of taxation. As we go back we find that records have a tendency to decrease and to concern smaller and smaller groups of people.

67. How many people can claim Norman descent in England?

A very large proportion of the population, if we reckon that Norman blood over the nine centuries since the Con-quest has permeated the nation. But if you mean who are the people who can say truthfully that their ancestors were at Hastings, they can be numbered on the fingers of one hand. The families of the Giffards and the Malets in the *Landed Gentry* and the Gresleys of Drakelowe in the *Peerage*, with De Marris again in *Landed Gentry*, and we have filled up the number of persons whose ancestor was at Hastings. I refer here of course to descent in the male line. There are also a number – possibly 200 – of families which are Norman but whose ancestor was not at Hastings, or at least not known to be. Such families as Curzon are unquestionably Norman, but I think it most doubtful that the original ancestor was at Hastings. We simply have not the records to prove or disprove it, but generally those who profit most in upheavals are not the hardy fighters who first go over the top.

68. What of pre-Conquest descent?

This is even rarer than Norman and for an obvious reason. The conquered either fled to other countries, or went under cover. Consequently it is only when a lucky find shows a Norman name at the beginning of what is otherwise a Norman-looking pedigree that we realize the essential native quality of some of our great houses. The FitzWilliams and the Berkeleys are cases in point, for both of them are native English in origin.

69. Why are so many people keen to have Norman blood?

A good point because it is does seem strange to want to come from a set of hoodlums, whose only difference from Hitler's Nazis was that they were more successful. However, there it is, the worship of success is very strong, and most English people want to be with the best people, whether they are alive or dead. Hence the wish for Norman ancestry, though bless the hearts of most of the would-be twentieth-century Normans, they are innocent of any connection with them.

70. What is the longest pedigree known?

Possibly that of the Emperor of Ethiopia. His descent is said by tradition to come from the marriage of the Queen of Sheba and King Solomon. This must have occurred about 1000 B.C., but there is no documentary evidence for the matter. However, in the fourth century A.D. the tradition was alive, and that is older than the oldest of the European monarchies. In Japan the line of the Mikado is reputed to go back to ages far lost in time. Even if we accept only the historically ascertainable line of the Mikados, it will stretch into the early Middle Ages, but I think that the principle of adoption has been brought into the family of the Japanese emperors as with the Romans so that one cannot reckon their pedigree as a contender in the lists of ancientry. In China some families claim descent from Confucius, according to one account amounting to as many as 40,000 persons. Confucius lived 2,500 years ago, so that if these claims are well founded, these Chinese pedigrees should be the oldest in the world.

71. What of European pedigrees?

There are all sorts of stories about Italian princes whose ancestry remounts to the later period of the Roman Empire; it may be so, but I do not think it can be proved. I well recall an occasion at one of the international congresses on genealogy which I attended, and at which an Italian expert put forward a motion that no pedigree should be accepted which went back earlier than the twelfth century. The only exceptions to this would be in the case of some of the royal families. The pedigree of Earl Mountbatten begins traditionally with an Earl Ydulf in the sixth century. A connected line is traced from Gislebert, ruler over what is now Belgium in the year 841. This corresponds very much to the line of ancestry of Her Majesty the Queen. The latter is traced back through Egbert of Wessex (who died in 839), and beyond him to Cerdic, King of Wessex, who like most of the Saxon royal lines traced his ancestry back to Wotan. The last-named apparently lived in the third century A.D.

However, once we have passed over these royal lines we can readily admit that the noble houses of Europe are as much bounded by the darkness of the early Middle Ages, as are our own distinguished families.

72. What do you think of the stories about Irish families going back into a very far time?

I take what I know is a reasonable standpoint with regard to Irish pedigrees. If you look them up in some books, such as the well-known O'Hart's *Irish Pedigrees*, you will find the lines of the various royal houses of Ireland traced back to Noah. For this reason what are called Milesian pedigrees (so named from a man named Milesius, King of Ireland about 1000 B.C.), have been laughed at for a long time. However, the considered judgement of scholars is that the two or three generations in a pedigree immediately before St. Patrick landed in Ireland (A.D. 432), can be taken as genuine. In any event they are strings of names which could easily be handed down by oral tradition. If this is the case a pedigree for an Irishman of the old royal lines could be correct back to approximately A.D. 400. After the time of St. Patrick, writing and Latin letters spread across Ireland, and the traditions began to be written down with the inevitable result that they were corrupted. The record of the generations nearest to St. Patrick's time would be the least corrupted. Such is the modern theory, and I can see no reason to doubt it. Ireland never had a kingship in the sense of Scotland's or England's central monarchy. There were four Irish provinces with kings of their own, and among these a high king or Ard Righ would be elected, in other words he proved the strongest. The pedigrees of these kings from about A.D. 400 are not doubtful. Before that date it is quite probable that they are genuine but we do not know and cannot prove or disprove. For the ascription of the Irish royal lines to the Biblical patriarchs we must remember that such was the practice in most western European countries after they became Christian. The line of the local kings was traced from the gods, and this line, gods and all was tacked on to the genealogies in the Old Testament.

73. What about the long Welsh pedigrees?

Here again we have a traditional element of some importance. Until the time of Henry VIII (himself half a Welshman) in 1542 English law did not apply to Wales. From 1542 England and Wales have been one entity with the same laws applicable to both. Before that date, Welsh law prevailed and under Welsh law the property of the father had to be divided equally among his sons. This meant a great deal of economic misery but it did promote genealogy. A man had to be ready to carry half a dozen generations of his family names in his mouth. He had to show who he was and that readily, so that he used the word 'ap' meaning 'son of'. He was, e.g. Rhys ap Tudor ap Morgan ap Griffith, ap Sais, ap Morgan, with 150 years of pedigree available at a moment's notice. This sort of thing promoted long memories of family history and many Welshmen could recite perfectly genuine pedigrees far longer than the half-dozen generations I have postulated here. In fact, as among the Highland Scots, there were officials whose duty it was to memorize the genealogies of the great men, the princes and kings. Consequently when one understands the nature of Welsh pedigrees one ceases to doubt their authenticity, for who would want to invent long lists of names merely for the sake of doing so.

74. You seem to place some value on tradition, do you think it is of use?

Yes and no. It depends entirely upon the place and the time. In some places such as old Ireland, or in Wales, the value of tradition is great. But in countries where a great store has been set on documentary history, or where there is a long tradition of learning, the value of tradition is greatly lessened. This applies to England. I think that before the Norman Conquest (1066) there were many traditional pedigrees which were recited by bards or handed down in tradition in families and that if the Normans had not overthrown so much of the English tradition, these pedigrees could have been handed down very much as in Wales or Ireland. As it happened the Normans broke the tradition and after some while a quite new standard arose. For many centuries England has had a literate class among her nobles, and where there are documents there is much less reliance upon tradition and oral remembrance, so that a tradition which appears in England in the fifteenth, sixteenth, or seventeenth centuries has very much less value than among more primitive peoples.

75. When you were the editor of *Burke's Peerage* you had the reputation of being a great wrecker of pedigrees; is this correct?

Not by any means, though as soon as it is announced that you have drastically revised some pedigrees, you will get the fame of being a pedigree breaker. In actual fact by my work at Burke's I was able to build up many pedigrees which otherwise would have continued to appear in the volume with an abbreviated account for the particular family. I did remove a large quantity of legends and myths, for which no adequate foundation could be provided.

76. What is the oldest pedigree in England?

The longest documented pedigree now known in England is that of the Arden family. This is a pedigree blessed by the great scholar J. H. Round – himself always accounted a great iconoclast – and who says of the Arden family tree: 'It had not only a clear descent from Aelfwine, Sheriff of Warwickshire in days before the Conquest, but even held, of the great possessions of which Domesday shows us its ancestor as lord, some manors which had been his before the Normans landed, at least as late as the days of Queen Elizabeth.' This is high praise from so great a genealogist, and it enables the Arden family to rank as the only English pedigree with a certainty of going back before the Conquest. There are others which are almost equally certain but where no absolute documentary proof can be found. These include the Berkeleys (in Scotland Barclays) whose descent from Eadnoth the Staller is almost beyond cavil. Eadnoth was killed in some fighting near Bristol in 1068. He was called the Staller as being a chamberlain to Edward the Confessor and evidently he transferred his allegiance to the Conqueror. Then there is the great Scottish family of Swinton whose ancestor is considered to have been the Edulfing or ruler of the district between the Tyne and the Forth in the days of Alfred the Great. Like many English families who did not care for the rule of William the Conqueror they migrated northward and were welcomed by the Scottish kings. In addition to these we can add the name of Wilberforce, famous in connection with one of its members, William Wilberforce who led the anti-slavery movement in Great Britain. This family claims a descent from a hardy soldier who had the distinction of fighting both at Stamford Bridge and at Hastings. When we have gone over this short list of four we have run over the families of England whose ancestry is pre-Conquest. The Ardens have a distinction of even greater fame. They produced Mary Arden, the mother of William Shakespeare. It seems peculiarly appropriate that the greatest of English poets should have been born of a family of undoubted English pre-Conquest stock.

77. What is the oldest pedigree in Scotland?

I should plump for the pedigree of the Earls of Mar. No date can be given for the origin of this earldom, and some of the greatest authorities describe the Earls of Mar as having been earls *ab initio*. The reason for this is that the original earls were known as the Mormaers or rulers of Mar, and after the Scottish kings extended their rule over the country, these Mormaers submitted to the crown and were known as Earls of Mar. The charter in which they are described as Earls of Mar is dated as early as 1114, and it was long before this that they had exercised power and authority in the mormaership. The family name is Erskine; the present holder of the title appears in peerage books as the 29th earl.

Scotland's history supplies many names of great families and it would be a difficult task to assign pre-eminence among them on the score of ancestry. The original people are generally called Celts, and among these we must place the Highland clans, a different race entirely from the lowlanders. There are many traditions of interest among the Highland clans, but in actual pedigree we do not get instances which correspond in length to those of their Celtic kinsmen in Wales and Ireland. For the great lowland families which often go back to the twelfth century in their authentic pedigrees, their origin is diverse. Some like the Haigs are probably Norman. Some are of English origin as Swinton is thought to be. There are even instances from farther afield. A very ancient tradition in the family of Drummond derives their origin from Hungary. Maurice who is reckoned as their progenitor came to Scotland with Edgar Atheling who had been born in Hungary and whose sister Margaret married King Malcolm Canmore in 1068. Hence the Dukes of Perth. In the earlier days of the Scottish kingdom, Scotland provided a good field of enterprise for ambitious men who found their own country for one reason or another unsuitable for them. In this way both dispossessed Englishmen and their Norman counterparts became Scots, and settled down in their new country; the Barclays for one thing are only the Berkeleys gone north. So too the Montgomeries were originally a great Norman family, a branch of which went north to found the earldom of Eglinton and Winton.

78. What is the longest pedigree in Wales?

There are about half a dozen Welsh pedigrees which have a millennium of family history behind them. One of the most interesting is that of Lord St. Davids. This used to appear in *Burke's Peerage* showing a descent from one Maximus, who had made himself Emperor of Britain in the 4th century, he being a Roman governor of Britain who had rebelled against his Emperor at Rome. Also brought into the pedigree account was Vortigern, the unlucky British king who was responsible for bringing the Saxons into Britain. This would have given Viscount St. Davids a pedigree as long, if not longer than, that of Her Majesty the Queen. In modern versions the family history begins modestly enough with a mere 900 years of ancestry. However, it is fact that as far back as the tenth century there had been a tradition in the family of descent from Maximus or Vortigern; so that at least a family capable of having such a tradition must have been anciently recorded as far back as a millennium ago.

Others of interest in Wales, and about the same age as the Philipps family (the surname of Viscount St. Davids) are Williams-Wynn; Lloyd-Davies; and Vaughan of Nannau. None of these families show a descent of less than some 900 years, and in all probability if traditional pedigrees are accepted, they could be taken much farther back.

79. What about the longest Irish pedigrees?

In my reply to question 72 I indicated my outlook with regard to Irish pedigrees, and my belief that many of the princely lines could be retraced to about A.D. 400. Among these one would certainly reckon the O'Conor Don; Mc-

Loughlin (Maelseachlainn); MacCarthy (Kings of Munster); O'Kelly of Gallagh; O'Briens and O'Neills. Full details of these very interesting pedigrees are to be found in books such as *Burke's Landed Gentry of Ireland*. Indeed it was through my occupation in bringing out a new edition of this work in 1958 (the last issue had been in 1912) that I was able to study many Irish pedigrees.

80. You referred to the Highlanders; what is the position with regard to the clan system, is there really a blood relationship in the main clan lines?

I should say very definitely, No, to the question, but such an answer requires some elaboration and explanation. If you look in books dealing with the Scottish clan system, such as the present Lord Lyon's revision of Frank Adams's *Clans, Septs and Regiments of the Scottish Highlands,* you will find between the lines quite a distinction between the family of the chief, such as the Mackintosh, or the McNab, and those who bear his name. If you search farther and look up the pedigrees of the chiefs in the *Peerage* or the *Landed Gentry,* you will see that the chief's pedigree is given there in detail, but there are no signs of connections of descent for all bearing his name. In the parlance of the genealogists, the chief is the eponymous, the name founder of the clan. I do not question the descent of the various chiefs, more than I would query the descent of any other notable family; but I do question very greatly the idea that, for instance, all Macphersons are connected by blood with the chief of Cluny Macpherson. I think it much more likely that in the early days of the clan, there were besides the family of the chief, branches of his line which occupied a more and more lowly position; in addition to these truly blood members, there were many persons who wanted protection and who joined themselves to the clan and took the name of the chief, as being his men. In fact we can find plenty of instances where such things did occur, and where broken men, i.e. persons whose own clan had suffered disaster, joined up with a more successful clan and took its name. This will account for the enormous number of Macs in the world, whose connection with the chief of their name is not even tenuous; it does not exist.

I would, however, make one exception to this observation, and that would be with the MacGregors. This clan, as is well known, was subjected to severe persecution during the seventeenth and eighteenth centuries; indeed during the years 1603–61 and 1693–1774 they were not allowed to use their own surname. For instance, the famous Rob Roy lived all his life as an outlaw in the eyes of the law. Yet when the ban on the MacGregors was lifted, 826 persons came forward to name their chief and to acknowledge themselves as MacGregors.

Another point is, that if the idea of all members of the clan being blood relations is untrue, it yet serves a marvellous purpose. It helps the ordinary Scotsman who perhaps cannot trace beyond his great-grandfather, to feel that he descends from men of fame, whose exploits are recorded in the annals of the clan, i.e. in the annals of the chief's family. Had such an idea of clanship occurred to the Smiths, Jones, Browns, and Robinsons, how much stronger would English social life and feeling be.

81. How do the Heralds' Visitations help with genealogy?

I referred to the Visitations in England and Wales in the answers to questions 15 and 34, but I will now be more specific about the genealogical side of these visits. The prime purpose was not to compile family history information. This resulted from the Heralds' Visitations as a side-line which became very important. For their own purposes, the visiting heralds would draw up rudimentary pedigrees; these were enlarged as generations passed, and copies were kept in the

College of Arms. Gradually it became a function of the heralds to maintain pedigrees, and this is one of the main features of their work today. As to the value of the Visitation pedigrees themselves, they are almost beyond calculation. If you can hitch yourself on to one of these pedigrees, you are genealogically home and dry.

82. What about entries in family Bibles, have they any value?

Yes, they often contain a considerable amount of information and should be scrutinized most carefully. They were used to record names of members of the family with their vital statistics, of birth, marriage and death, and sometimes other incidents in their lives.

I should also strongly suggest or urge would-be seekers after family history to ask any aged relatives they have for details about the family. I have known an old member of a family keep something to himself for a long time, and then suddenly burst out with it, to the great surprise of a younger person. 'Why didn't you tell me of this before?' is a very natural inquiry, and it is usually answered with, 'Well, I never thought that you would be interested in it.' In such a way, I for one, learned of the existence of a relationship with some Sayer cousins, whose names in connection with my own genealogy had puzzled me for some time. Therefore if you have older members of the family, pump them for information. Remember that the day will come when you will be able to learn nothing more from their lips.

83. What exactly is cousinship?

It is much more difficult for us to use the word 'cousin' or 'kinsman' than it was for our ancestors. If anyone reads Shakespeare's plays or other documents of the sixteenth–seventeenth centuries, he will find the use of the word 'cousin' very frequent. It is a very simple and useful word, for once one has passed from the immediate family circle, or outside the range of aunts, uncles, grandparents, etc., what else is a man or woman to be called, but cousin or kinsman or kinswoman. With the latter words, too, our ancestors were much more liberal and sensible than we are. They recognized kinship and did not try to work out exact details where this was not too easy. The formal definition of 'cousin' is of course that of the son or daughter of an uncle or aunt. Cousin-german means simply first cousin; those who like can work out all the grades of first cousin twice removed, second cousin and the rest of it. Simply to refer to a person as 'kinsman' is simpler. Often with pedigrees in days gone by we know that a relationship existed between two men, but we cannot define it exactly. Those who lived at the time knew quite well that they were related, and did not bother about exact places in the family tree. The use of the same arms would not be tolerated between persons who were not of the same blood, and hence heraldry greatly aided genealogy.

84. What is the truth about the millions of money lying in Chancery?

The truth is often very unpalatable to people who are hoping to get large fortunes out of Chancery. As a general rule there are no large sums lying in Chancery. A leaflet is issued by the Supreme Court Pay Office of the Royal Courts of Justice in London, which gives some very illuminating details about funds held in Chancery. It states that the majority of the funds are of small amounts, and it tells inquirers where they can get the information about such accounts as are held there. It also very significantly adds a warning against syndicates and agents professing to deal with millions of money held in Chancery for various families. It even gives the names of some of these alleged benefactors, such as Drake, Hyde, Page, Everingham and Bailey.

It is a tragic fact that there have been many people who have deluded themselves into thinking that huge sums of money are awaiting them in the Court of Chancery. I had one instance brought to my notice, in which a woman (in America) was under the impression that the city of London had belonged to her forebears, and that she had only to put in her claim to receive untold sums of money from the English courts. Anyone who thinks that there is something waiting for him or her in the Chancery Court should write to the Supreme Court Pay Office at the address given above.

85. Are there sums of money going with titles. e.g. of peers?

This is another delusion similar to the one dealt with in the answer to question 84. There are a few cases in which estates are entailed, i.e. settled on a series of heirs, so that the present owner is more like a tenant. In fact in the case of an entail, the owner in being is referred to as the tenant for life, and he has definite bounds set on his powers of dealing with the estate. Only in such a case where an estate is entailed and where the owner is a peer can there be said to be any money accompanying the peerage. These cases grow fewer every decade. In the vast majority of peerages, no money of any sort goes with the inheritance of the title as such. I have known many peers who have inherited a title only to find that they are not thereby relieved from the necessity of earning a living. They have the peerage but they have nothing beyond the honour of it. If this fact could be grasped by most people, there would not be so much seeking after peerages which are dormant, or in abeyance.

86. What are peerages dormant or in abeyance?

A dormant peerage is where it is known, or at least thought that an heir exists, but where the heir has not come forward to prove his title. An abeyant peerage is one in which the succession to the title cannot be proved until a male heir emerges from among the female heirs to a title. E.g. a peer dies, and the peerage is said to lie in abeyance between his daughters, until one of them produces a male heir, or rather until from their lines emerges a single male heir. An abeyancy can be terminated by the sovereign if he or she feels so inclined.

87. How should one start to trace Welsh ancestry?

Your best beginning is to go to the Honourable Society of Cymmrodorion, 20 Bedford Square, London, W.C.1. If you join this society you will find many persons whose interests are in common with yours and who would help you. You will realize that from 1542 Wales and England are administratively one, and that what applies to English records from that time will apply to Welsh records also. Only if you think that you can get back behind 1542 will the wealth of Welsh genealogical material help you.

88. How should one trace Irish ancestry?

Get in touch with the Chief Herald of Ireland, Dublin Castle, Ireland. He will help you from the store of records under his keeping, but will also direct you to places where you can consult genealogical records in Ireland. Remember, however, as I have mentioned before that much of the most valuable of the Irish family history went up in smoke in 1922.

89. What about Northern Ireland?

Yes, unfortunately genealogy must take account of political differences. It would be so much easier if we could ignore them and get on with the sensible task of tracing a man's ancestry whether he belonged to the Republic or the

North. However, there it is, and if you want ancestry in Northern Ireland, you had better get in touch with the Registrar-General, the General Register Office, Fermanagh House, Ormean Avenue, Belfast. There is a Public Record Office, too, and this is in May Street, Belfast; you would contact the Deputy Keeper. For those of Presbyterian backgrounds, write to the Secretary, Church House, Belfast.

90. One last question on genealogy, do you think it is of any real value?

St. Paul warned his spiritual sons, Timothy and Titus against it, and he was used to it. Yet there have been times recently when genealogical knowledge could be a matter of life and death, in Hitler's Germany where the possession of a great-grandmother of Jewish blood spelt imprisonment, perhaps death. Between these two extremes comes the quiet study of one's predecessors, who they were, what they did; perhaps the recovery of some precious letter or a will from the centuries dust in which it has lain, and from those faded pages a man or woman steps forth, without whom we ourselves should never have been.

3

Titles

91. Is a retiring premier made an earl?

This is only a custom, but custom does acquire great force. The practice for some time past has been to offer a premier when he retires the choice of an earldom. Since the war two of our six prime ministers have accepted an earldom, Sir Anthony Eden as Earl of Avon, and Mr. Attlee as Earl Attlee. Mr. Macmillan has declined the offer, and so it is believed did Sir Winston Churchill.

92. What could happen in the case of Sir Alec Douglas-Home who gave up his earldom in order to become premier?

Many people think that when Sir Alec retires from political life he would simply be offered an earldom, and thus perhaps get his old earldom of Home back again. This is the popular impression which one gathers from conversations on trains and in shops, etc. In fact it is quite wrong, because under the Peerage Act of 1963, there is a definite statement [sec. 3 (2)] that a person who has disclaimed a peerage under the Act shall not receive any other hereditary peerage. It is true that this does not bar out the conferring of a life peerage, but a life earldom is something quite out of the ordinary and I doubt if this would be created. It looks therefore as if Sir Alec would have to be remaining as a commoner, after he leaves the Commons, whenever that may be.

93. What is meant by the Peerage Act 1963?

This Act is popularly known as the Wedgwood Benn enabling Act, because it was principally brought about by the exertions of Mr. Wedgwood Benn who inherited the peerage of Stansgate but who did not want to take it, as it meant him giving up his career in the House of Commons where he was sitting as an M.P. The Act, however, does much more than this, for it removes several strange anomalies which have lasted for a long time. It allows Scottish peers to sit in the House, whereas previously only those Scottish peers who were elected as representative peers, or had a United Kingdom peerage in addition to their Scots peerage, were allowed to do so. It also allows peeresses in their own right to sit in the Lords. It did not touch the position of Irish peers. Formerly the Irish peers were allowed to elect 28 of their number to sit in the House of Lords for life, and those peers who were not so elected were able to stand for seats in the Commons. Since 1921 when the Irish Free State was formed no elections of Irish peers have taken place, and there are since 1961 (when the Earl of Kilmorey died) no more representative peers for Ireland.

94. What is the Life Peerage Act?

This Act was passed in 1958 to allow for the creation of life peers, both men and women, the object being to alter the balance in the House of Lords so that a more democratic element should enter into the Upper House. This has not really been effective, because since 1958 just as many hereditary peerages have been created as life peerages. Consequently although there are more life peers in the House than there were – previous to 1958 the only life peers were the Law Lords – the proportion of life peers to hereditary who do attend the debates remains fairly constant. By allowing the creation of women life peers the objection to the peeresses in their own right was removed and this has now been put in order by the 1963 Peerage Act. Other changes have taken place in the House of Lords over the last few years; pay in the form of three guineas a day was introduced for those peers who attended at the House, for each day of attendance; and peers who do not want to take part in the business of the Lords are now allowed to apply to be excused from receiving the writ of summons.

95. Would the creation of life peerages only, be sufficient to reform the House of Lords?

This subject of reform of the Lords has been canvassed on and off ever since the passing of the Parliament Act 1911, when in the preamble to the Act it was stated that House of Lords 'reform brooked no delay.' In fact the substitution of life peers for hereditary would have one good effect, it would prevent the creation for the future of pauper peers. It does not need much reflection to realize that with our present system of heavy taxation, the handing on of money in large investments becomes increasingly difficult, and therefore within a generation or so, the heirs of a wealthy peer are often very hard up. Nor is it hard to think of instances within the last decade in which some very unbecoming behaviour, on the part of peers, occasioned by poverty, has been brought to light. But apart from a socially good result, the life peerage idea does not really reform the House of Lords; indeed paradoxically it is to hereditary peerages that we must look for the appearance of bright young men of ability. Most life peers are men and women of 60 years of age or thereabouts, and they have usually settled down to an established mode of life. Conversely the young heir to an old peerage may be full of ideas for progress. Consequently I think – it is purely my idea – that the House of Lords can only be reformed by taking it right out of the legislature, and by substituting for it a body similar to the American or Australian senate, which would be elective. I do not, however, advocate the abolition of titles, which do no harm to anyone, except sometimes their possessor.

96. Can you give up a title in favour of someone else?

No. My postbag has often contained letters from people who state that some forebear of theirs gave up his baronetcy or peerage in favour of someone else. This is all nonsense, and there is no truth in it. It may be noted, too, that under the 1963 Peerage Act, the fact that a peer has renounced his peerage does not accelerate the succession of his heir.

97. How do you put in a claim to a peerage or baronetcy?

By applying to the Home Secretary, the Home Office, Whitehall, London. You will be required to put in some extensive information in order to prove a claim, unless of course it is purely formal, as when a son claims to succeed to his father's peerage or baronetcy.

98. Why do so many titles in England become extinct?

I can only conclude that there must be an excessive failure in peers as opposed to other men to produce male heirs. Certain it is that the wastage in the peerage is very great, though it is much more than made good, as anyone can see if they study the Rolls of the Lords produced each autumn by the Stationery Office. These Rolls always show an increase in numbers. However, it is a strange fact that while peerages often become extinct, baronetcies do not, but an heir to a baronetcy turns up in some out of the way part of the world. It could also be added that the following illustrious names are no longer represented in the male line: Shakespeare, Milton, Marlborough (Churchill), Nelson, Sir Walter Scott, Chatham (Pitt), Edmund Burke, Fox, Canning, Macaulay, Palmerston, or Disraeli.

99. Can a foreigner who becomes a British subject retain his title or coat of arms?

Strictly speaking, no. In fact there are quite a number of people who are British subjects and who still use their countships or other foreign titles; certainly there are many foreign coats of arms in use in England. The principle is that the sovereign of the country is the source or Fountain of Honours, and she or he can grant or withhold whatever honours it may please them. There has also been from the time of Queen Elizabeth I a strong disinclination, to put it no higher, on the part of our kings and queens to permit the use of foreign titles by their subjects. Papal titles are right outside, and the regulation of those which are of secular origin, comes under a Royal Warrant issued by King George V in 1932. This Warrant lays down the principle that in due course the use of foreign titles shall cease in England and permits only a relatively few to British subjects.

100. What is the position of Canadians, Australians and so on who are offered British titles?

The subject is a sore one, for nowadays the fine old principle that one was a British subject anywhere in the Queen's dominions does not apply. People are Canadians, New Zealanders, Australians, Trinadadians, etc., and only those who are subjects of the United Kingdom can properly be classed as British. Moreover, many if not all of the old Dominions have decided against the acceptance of hereditary titles by their nationals. The acceptance of a peerage for instance by Mr. Roy Thomson, now Lord Thomson of Fleet, is said to be likely to involve him in difficulties with the Canadian legal position if and when he returns to Canada. For some thirty years now Canada has set itself against the acceptance by its nationals of honours, of the titled variety at least. One has only to look through the lists in the New Year's or Birthday Honours to see that very few parts of the old Empire are now represented. In the last Birthday Honours List there are sections for the colonies which are still ruled from Whitehall or still fairly closely connected with this country; there are sections also for Australia and New Zealand, but even in the latter cases they are only for non-hereditary honours.

Gradually then or perhaps one could say swiftly the scope of the Lists is being restricted to the United Kingdom.

101. Is it correct to style a British peer a Baron, e.g. Baron Beaverbrook?

Baron is a designation of the lowest order in the peerage, but it should not be used in English except in very formal documents. It is certainly wrong to refer to anyone as Baron Robens if he holds a British title. It is correct to refer to Baron de Reuter, since his is a foreign title which he is permitted by Royal Warrant to use. All the other grades of the peerage – viscount, earl, marquess and duke – are correctly so-called. However, it is common form to refer to all peers under the rank of Duke as Lord.

102. Is the form correct – namely the Lord X?

Yes, in formal documents, or even on letters if you want to be very correct, but nothing could be more out of place than to refer to The Lord Rank for example in an account of some sporting event in which he had taken part. The

F   81

form The Lord X should be used, if at all apart from formal letters, only on envelopes addressed by strangers.

103. Is it right to put Rt. Hon. before the names of peers?

Yes, this matter was thrashed out some years ago. The usage of putting Right Honourable before the names of peers spread from the days – about 400 years ago – when the few peers who then existed were all members of the Privy Council. From this the habit spread on to the whole of the peerage below the rank of marquess. There was a controversy about it some years back, but it was settled by a ruling from Garter King of Arms that Right Hon. was right.

104. How is a lady to be addressed who has been married to a titled man, then divorced and married to an untitled man?

A woman's title derives from her husband or father as does her surname. Consequently a woman who has married a titled person takes the corresponding title due to his wife. Thus Miss X becomes the countess of Y on marriage to the Earl of Y. But on divorce from the Earl, the relationship has ended, and so the title can only be used as long as the former wife does not marry again. When she does, she takes the title of her new husband. If he is a plain mister, then her title is Mrs. It frequently happens that a woman having had a divorce, and married again, feels that she wants to keep her former title and does so. This is wrong and should definitely be discouraged by all concerned.

105. When a man has been knighted, may he be addressed as 'Sir'?

Only after he has received the accolade, that is had the sword-tip laid on his shoulder. Until then he is correctly

1. EARL

2. MARQUESS

Fig. 5 – CORONETS OF RANK

referred to as 'Mr.' Letters of congratulation should be so addressed. The same principle holds with a peer, except that his period of waiting, between acceptance of a peerage and actual peerage style, is ended by the official entry in the *London Gazette*. The new peer's style cannot be known until it has been officially settled by entry in the *Gazette*, so it would be a serious solecism to address him as Lord X before we can know how he is to be entitled. In the case of a baronet, it is possible to address him as Sir William X as soon as it has been announced that he is to be made a baronet. The reason is that he is not likely to ask to change his surname when he has got his baronetcy, and so we can call him Sir William X, since the only addition which the *Gazette* will add to that will be 'of Tower Green Hamlets, etc.' or whatever territorial designation he is going to take.

106. What position does a foreign duke have in this country?

This is purely a matter of politeness, and the same thing applies to other foreign titles. As a general rule a foreign duke would take precedence behind the British dukes. Obviously his position in his own country must be a recognized one.

107. How can one check on a foreign title?

This is difficult. In a great many continental countries the monarchy has gone, and this means that the official check on the nobility has gone too. As a result it has become very hard to check a foreign title. There are some books which might be useful to a searcher, such as the *Libro d'Oro* of Italy, which gives particulars of noble families. There is not likely, however, to be in any, except a few continental countries, any official check list such as we possess in the House of Lords, the Home Office and the College of Arms. The best thing to do if the matter is one of importance, is to consult the embassy of the country concerned.

1. DUKE

2. ROYAL DUKE
(e.g. Sovereign's Grandchildren, or sons of Sovereign's brothers)

Fig. 6 – CORONETS OF RANK

108. What are courtesy titles?

These are the secondary titles of peers which are used by their sons out of courtesy. No subject seems to exercise more difficulty than this one. Yet if one thinks about it, it is quite simple. Consider the titles borne by the Duke of Marlborough. He is beside his dukedom, Marquess of Blandford, Earl of Sunderland, Earl of Marlborough, Baron Spencer and Baron Churchill. Clearly the Duke cannot use all these titles at once. It therefore seems quite in order for his eldest son to be styled by his father's best secondary title. Thus the Duke's son is called out of courtesy, the Marquess of Blandford. He is not a peer, and being a commoner, can stand for and sit in the House of Commons. Courtesy titles are found in each rank of the peerage, but they are only recognizable as peerage titles when they belong to earldoms, marquessates or dukedoms. A Viscount may be also a baron, but even so his eldest son will be called the Hon. The latter is also a courtesy title, but is not a peerage dignity. With earls, it is very unlikely that they will not possess a secondary or even tertiary peerage; the theory is that a man was advanced through various grades until he reached the dignity of an earl. Thus today anyone created an earl, is likely or almost certain to have a viscounty conferred on him also.

109. Which is correct – "marquess" or "marquis"?

The latter is a foreign form, and the former is the English variant. The former should therefore be used.

110. What should be the style of the grandson of a duke or marquess?

Plain mister is enough, but nowadays the custom is to give one of the courtesy titles to the grandson. A case in

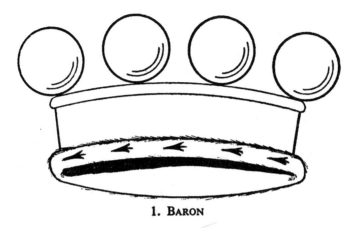

1. BARON

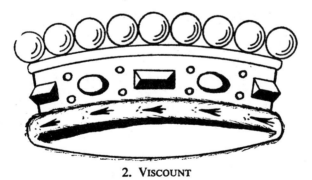

2. VISCOUNT

Fig. 7 – CORONETS OF RANK

point is that of the Earl of Sunderland, the son of the Marquess of Blandford, himself the son of the Duke of Marlborough. It is purely a matter of custom, nothing more.

111. Is the term dowager ever used now?

It is still found occasionally but very rarely does a widowed peeress describe herself as a dowager. The style used most frequently is to put the Christian name of the lady before her rank. Thus, Mary, Lady Petworth, instead of the Dowager Lady Petworth. This habit of using the Christian name, apparently began far back in the reign of Queen Victoria and is now well established.

112. What is the difference between a diocesan bishop and a suffragan bishop?

A diocesan bishop holds sway over a see in which he is the sole responsible bishop. He is styled correctly the Lord Bishop of London. A suffragan bishop holds his position under the rule of a diocesan bishop whom he is appointed to assist. He is of course a bishop, but he should never be styled Lord Bishop; his correct style is Right Rev. A.Y.Z., Bishop of X. Suffragans have no official place or precedence.

113. You refer to precedence, what exactly is it and how is it regulated?

Precedence is governed by an Act of Parliament, the title of which – for the placing of the lords – explains what it is about. This Act still governs the rules of ordering those persons who are to be present on official occasions. As may be imagined it has had to be altered or amended many times, for it was passed in the reign of Henry VIII (in 1539).

It did not include the Prime Minister, since at that time no such office existed. Indeed until 1905 there was no official place for the Prime Minister in the Table of Precedence; he found a place as First Lord of the Treasury. To this day such notable office holders as the Lord Mayor of London, or the Cardinal Archbishop of Westminster may be sought in vain in the list of V.I.P.s, though the Table does find place for Esquires and Gentlemen. Since the last war the High Commissioners of the great Dominions such as Canada, or Australia have been given the precedence and place accorded to Ambassadors of sovereign States. This Table is used on high State occasions, but it has often proved unhelpful to harassed secretaries of organizations when some great dinner is being staged. For once one is outside the circle of the truly great of the land, there is some remarkable difficulty in finding out exactly how to place one's guests without giving offence.

114. What is the precedence among foreign sovereigns?

This means the precedence of sovereigns who are visiting the court of St. James's. The answer is very short, all sovereigns are viewed as being equal in rank, as sovereigns, and their precedence is determined by their dates of accession. This situation could formerly have been very serious, when many monarchies existed in Europe. It is not of great importance now.

115. What do the letters C.D. mean on a car?

Corps Diplomatique. They have an almost magical power, and can ensure the rightful user of them of a vast range of immunity. As he represents a foreign sovereign power, he cannot be made subject to the usual procedure of the courts of this realm. If he commits some crime or falls into some civil legal difficulty, he cannot be sued or prosecuted, and

Fig. 8. BADGE OF BARONET (United Kingdom)

the only redress is to request the government which he represents to withdraw him from Britain. This immunity applies not only to the ambassador or to the first or second secretary but also to many members of the staff of an embassy if not to all. It springs in England, from a commotion in the reign of Queen Anne, when an ambassador was illtreated by a mob. It is, whatever its abuse on occasion, a valuable privilege of civilized life.

116. What is the surname of the royal family?

Windsor. In 1917 King George V issued a proclamation declaring that the name of Windsor is to be borne by his royal house and family and relinquishing the use of all German titles and dignities. This continued until the death of George VI in 1952 and the accession of Her Majesty the Queen. At the time of her accession the Queen bore the surname of Mountbatten, this being her husband's name. On 9th April, 1952, the Queen signified her pleasure that from henceforth she and her children should be styled as the House and Family of Windsor, and that her descendants other than female descendants who marry, and their descendants, should bear the name of Windsor. By a later warrant the Queen went so far as to allow the use of Mountbatten–Windsor for certain descendants in the distant future, three or more generations away (by declaration of 8 February, 1960, 'descendants who will enjoy neither the style, title or attribute of Royal Highness, nor the titular dignity of Prince and for whom therefore a surname will be necessary,' i.e. a younger grandchild of Prince Charles). This is the first time that a hyphenated surname has been used in our royal family. However, if we go back before 1917 it was the considered opinion of that great genealogical scholar Sir Bernard Burke that the royal family had no surname. Writing of Queen Victoria he said: 'I feel persuaded that the Royal House of Saxe-Coburg has no surname. When the adoption of surnames became general, the ancestors of that illustrious race were Kings, and needed no other designation than the Christian name added to the Royal title.' Some have contended for Guelph, or Welf, but in 1917 when George V asked the College of Arms for his royal surname there was no considered opinion opposed to that of Sir Bernard Burke.

117. Is there any means of checking foreign decorations and orders?

The only way is to approach the embassy of the particular country and to inquire there. Often the embassy has not the specialized information. The members of the staff cannot be experts on everything, though one would expect them to understand their country's orders and decorations. Mostly they depend upon official statements. To be quite fair to the embassy staffs, in many countries there has been a change of régime, and orders which were formerly held in high esteem, are now out of fashion, and in fact sometimes dangerous to the owner, as marking him as a member of a bad government. There are few books on the subject of orders, and hardly anything which gives a full view of the whole field. How could this be, considering the vastness of the subject. As more and more states appear on the scene, as empires break up and independent countries come into being, the number of decorations continually increases. There are many completely 'phoney' orders which circulate, usually being bestowed for money. Anyone who is approached on this subject should at once ask for the name of the country concerned and consult its embassy. Whatever the extent of the embassy's knowledge on genuine orders, it will nearly always have the necessary information on false orders, since they do seriously lessen a country's prestige.

118. What is a morganatic marriage?

The popular idea is that it means a marriage in which a man of exalted rank gives his 'left' hand to a second wife, in other words a means whereby a man is able to have two wives at once. This is bunkum. The term morganatic marriage arose in Germany where a very high idea of rank has always prevailed, causing the usual amount of human suffering as a result. Among the exalted Teutonic conceptions of high breeding there came the idea that a man of royal position who wanted to get married to someone of lower social status, should indeed marry her, but that his wife should be excluded from his family name, his arms and title. The marriage is genuine and the children legitimate, but they too are excluded from inheriting their father's titles or the entailed property of the family. Their only inheritance is what may be settled on them by contract, and hence the term morganatic, since it is derived from the German *morgen-gave* meaning the gift from the bridegroom to the bride on the morning after the marriage. Many will recall the mention of this idea of a morganatic marriage in the case of the Duke of Windsor as a possible solution of his difficulties when as Edward VIII he wished to marry Mrs. Simpson. The idea was at once scouted as not being within the terms known to English law.

119. What is the Red Hand of Ulster?

This is the hand which appears on the badge of the baronets (except those of Nova Scotia, who have the royal arms of Scotland on the cross of St. Andrew). The Red Hand of Ulster has become familiar to many people from its appearance on the sign of a well-known brewery. The Red Hand was the badge of the old O'Neills, the ancient Kings of Ulster, who were driven out by the plantation of Ulster under King James I in 1611, when the order of baronets was instituted in order to pay for the settlement of Ulster. The hand as used by the baronets is not however the O'Neill badge, which was the right hand as the baronets use the left hand; the brewery does use the right hand.

120. What are the flags which are often seen flying over private houses in England, and which are not readily identifiable?

These are the flags of the owners of the houses, and which are their owners' arms. Cases in point which I have seen are those of Viscount Scarsdale over Kedleston House, of the Marquess of Bath over Longleat, and of Lord Montagu over Beaulieu. It is a picturesque and attractive sight and one which I hope will not die out in this country.

121. Can a baronet claim a knighthood for his eldest son?

He could until 1827, for on 19th December in that year, King George IV gave orders that in future a baronet's patent should not contain the clause which permitted his eldest son on attaining the age of 21 to be knighted. Previous to that a baronet whose patent of creation contained this clause could request the honour of knighthood for his eldest son when the latter became 21. This seems to have been a very curious habit, for why should a youth of 21 be made a knight just because his father was a baronet, whose title the young man would in the ordinary course of nature inherit? In addition when father and son bore the same Christian name there must have been a great confusion.

122. Who is the Deemster?

There are in the Isle of Man two judges or justices who are called Deemsters. The style used is His Honour the Deemster X (the latter being of course his surname). For over 150 years the Deemster has been socially and officially designated 'His Honour'. I am informed that in 1925 the question was raised as to the designation of a Deemster on his retirement. The Governor of the Isle of Man was notified by the Home Office that the title of His Honour may be retained by a Deemster after his retirement from office.

123. Who are the Bailiffs in the Channel Islands?

There are two in the Channel Islands, one in Jersey, and the other in Guernsey and its Dependencies. They are supreme civil officers in each case, and they preside at the royal court, also over the states parliament, and represent the Crown in all civil matters. The Bailiff of Guernsey is so styled and is addressed as Mr. Bailiff. The Bailiff of Jersey is styled as such and is written to as 'Dear Mr. Bailiff', while in address he is Mr. Bailiff. (Presumably the Bailiff of Guernsey would be addressed in writing as 'Dear Mr. Bailiff'.)

124. What is the style of a county court judge in England after retirement?

His style after retirement is, as during tenure, 'His Honour'; he is referred to as Judge X, though I am informed that this is by courtesy only, and that strictly he should be referred to as Mr. X.

125. What is the Clan Chattan?

Right at the beginning we may say that it is pronounced as Clan Hattan. It is an association or group of clans which comprehends the Macphersons, MacGillivrays, Farquharsons, MacQueens, Macfaills, Macbeans, and others. An account of it occurs in Sir Walter Scott's romance, *The Fair Maid of Perth*, though it must be admitted that Sir Walter in his quotations from old Scottish historians shows that the earlier authorities gave Clanwhewyl, and Clachinya, or Clanquhele and Clankay as the names of the two groups with whose fortunes his story is concerned. In other chronicles they became Clanquhele and Clankay, but Hector Boece, so Scott tells us, wrote of them as Clanchattan and Clankay. These two groups of clans had kept the Highlands in turmoil and disorder greater than usual until at last the authorities in Scotland had decided to arrange for them a combat to the death. This was to consist in thirty picked men on either side led by their chiefs fighting to death at Perth and this combat actually took place in 1396. It resulted in the victory of Clan Chattan, while the defeated Clan Kay broke up into minor groups.

However, this may have been embroidered in the hands

Fig. 9. – BADGE OF BARONET (Nova Scotia)

of the great romancer of the north, certain it is that Clan Chattan as a group of tribes held a dominant position in the Highlands in the time of Robert III of Scotland at the end of the fourteenth century. A Declaration of Lyon Court on 10th September, 1672, from the Lord Lyon gave the necessary details regarding the composition and headship of Clan Chattan. The Laird of Mackintosh is the only undoubted chief of the name of Mackintosh and the chief of Clan Chattan. None of the families of the other names mentioned will be given arms by the Lord Lyon except as cadets of the Laird of Mackintosh's family, because his predecessor married the heiress of the Clan Chattan in 1291. The chief of the clan has the name in Gaelic of Gillie-chattan Mor, which means the Great Servant of St. Catan.

This is thought to mean that originally the founder of the Clan was the bailie of the Abbey of Kilchattan, in Bute. No less than seventeen tribes are given as members of the Clan Chattan by the present Lord Lyon, Sir Thomas Innes of Learney in his revision of Frank Adams's book, *The Clans, Septs and Regiments of the Scottish Highlands.*

126. Is it correct to style a Scottish chief, The Mackintosh? etc.

Yes, it has been done since the fifteenth century, when there was a custom of styling some of the Lowland chiefs with 'Le' before their surname or title. Today the practice prevails of styling the chief of the whole name or clan as it is called, 'The'. Thus we have 'The Mackintosh', one of the most famous of all. This form is used in official records such as the Register of the Lord Lyon. As was noted in the answer to question 125, the chief of a great clan like Mackintosh can also be correctly styled Laird of Mackintosh, although it has been pointed out by Sir Thomas Innes that in this case the reference is not to a landed estate but to the clan or family of Mackintosh. A very common form of reference to these highland chiefs is in the style, Mac-Gregor of MacGregor, where the reduplication is meant to give greater distinction to the fact that it is to the chief that reference is made. In Scotland, both highland and lowland, the territorial designation is frequent, and so we get Urquhart of Cromarty, Cameron of Lochiel, etc. When the name of the property is the same as that of the family (a fairly frequent occurrence with very old recorded families), the words 'of that ilk' are often used, so that Udny of Udny could be rightly called Udny of that ilk.

Before passing on from the subject of chiefly designation, I cannot forbear to mention the case of the Chisholm chief, whose clan is not perhaps one of the most numerous. What it lacked in numbers it appeared to make up in importance, for of old, it was held by the clan that there were in the world only three persons of consequence, The Pope, The King and The Chisholm.

Readers of Scottish romances may be puzzled by the title Baron of –, as in the case of Sir Walter Scott's *Waverley* where he refers to the Baron of Bradwardine, though the latter is not a lord in our sense. According to Sir Thomas Innes, Lord Lyon, the title of Baron X etc. is a highland custom in place of the more usual Laird of X employed in the lowlands. He points out too that on the European continent the words laird (or baronet for that matter) are not understood, but Baron like Knight or Chevalier is.

127. What is the meaning of the Scottish expression 'of that ilk'?

It is a term used to designate the laird or possessor of an estate when the name of the estate and the surname of the family are identical. In the current *Landed Gentry*, of 1952, on page 2,459 there is a reference to Swinton of that ilk. On looking into the pedigree we see that the laird of Swinton is described as 33rd of that ilk, and the family history states that 'the family of Swinton takes its name from the lands of Swinton, which it has held for more than eight and a half centuries.'

See also answer to question 126.

128. What does the term 'younger' mean when applied to the name of a Scottish gentleman?

It denotes the heir apparent to a Scottish lairdship. Thus, my editor when first I became connected with *Burke's Landed Gentry* was Harry Pirie-Gordon the Younger, of Buthlaw, so styled because at that time his father was still alive. Today he is Pirie Gordon, 13th of Buthlaw. The numbering used here and in the answer to question 127 in the case of lairds is to denote that their territory is really an old feudal barony, that they are in short, Barons of X.Y.Z., etc. but not peers of course in the sense of being Lords of Parliament.

129. When then, is a Baron not a Baron?

As pointed out in the answer to question 101, a British Baron, i.e. a peer in the lowest order of the peerage is not styled Baron except in very official documents, but is addressed in speech and in normal writing as Lord X. A foreign Baron is correctly referred to as Baron X. The holder of a foreign barony whose right to use the title in England has not been granted by the Crown, i.e. a British subject who owns a foreign barony is in a very awkward position. If he styles himself Baron X, he is not likely to incur any penalties greater than those of being excluded from official gatherings at St. James's or Buckingham Palace. But if he allows newspaper reporters to refer to him as Lord X, he is in the position of appearing to be a peer of the realm which he is not. The life of such a person is fraught with difficult moments.

In the instance of Scottish Barons to which I have referred in questions 126 and 128, we deal with the idea of old feudal baronies, which went with the land. These baronies, might, but did not always, carry with them the right to a seat in Parliament. If they did, the owner of the feudal barony was also a lord of Parliament, and today the feudal barons of Scotland are only a relic, sentimental and interesting be it agreed, of the time before the passing of the Heritable Jurisdiction Act, 1746. For that matter no country can be more interesting to the student of history than Scotland, for it contains numerous relics of practices from feudal and heraldic times which have long since disappeared in England and elsewhere.

130. Is it true that anyone who buys Arundel Castle would become Duke of Norfolk?

No. In England in centuries now long past there were many cases, no doubt, of titles which went with the land, peerages by the tenure of certain properties, as they are termed in English law. They have no existence now. As long ago as 1819–22 the Redesdale Committee in their Reports upon peerage concluded that there were no peerages by the tenure existing at that time (1819), and that none had existed since the time of Henry III or Edward I (the latter sovereign reigned from 1272 to 1307). The conception of the feudal barony to which reference has been made in the case of Scotland (see above) does not exist in England.

131. What is the correct mode of address for the wife of a laird in Scotland?

In this respect I cannot do better than give you the view of the highest Scottish authority. The Lord Lyon in his *Scots Heraldry,* page 209 (1956 edition) says: 'Feudal rank is legally communicated to the wife, and a Laird's wife is legally "the Lady Lour". In rural Scotland, at any rate, this correct address (invariably used in the old Scottish Law Reports) is still in use.' Consequently the lady would be correctly addressed in writing as Madam, and referred to in speech as Lady X. In formal invitations in Scotland in recent years I have had notes from the Baron of Y and Madame Y. It is, however, much more frequent to refer to the wife of a laird as 'Mrs. X of Y' the Y being the name of the husband's estate.

132. Can the Order of the Garter be conferred upon a lady?

Yes, there are usually one or two Ladies of the Garter. At present there is the Queen Mother, who was made a

Fig. 10 – ARMORIAL COAT
showing—
Shield in "Cauché" position (slantwise)
Lambrequin, or mantling
Chapeau, or cap of estate

101

Lady of the Garter on 14th December, 1936, when she was the Queen Consort of King George VI. So, too, had the late Queen Mary been a Lady of the Garter from 3rd June, 1910, until her death. In addition among the list of additional knights, which is usually composed of foreign sovereigns, is the name of Princess Wilhelmina of the Netherlands. She was admitted a Lady of the Garter because she was a sovereign. Similarly the Sovereign of this country, whether King or Queen is always Sovereign of the Order of the Garter and of the other orders of chivalry of the United Kingdom. The Queen was admitted a Lady of the Order in 1948 at a solemn ceremonial which marked the 600th anniversary of the founding of the Order and at which her husband, the Duke of Edinburgh was also installed as a Knight.

Thus the number of ladies of the Order is much restricted to those who are of the highest royal rank. It was pointed out by Sir Bernard Burke that in the early days of the Order it was the custom for the wives and widows of the Knights of the Garter to wear the habit of the Order on the feast-days of St. George, and to be in fact Ladies of the Order. The habit died out in Tudor days, and was only revived in the present century, though the Garter is now of course much restricted in its bestowal on women as compared with medieval times.

133. Who and what is the Knight of Glin?

He is the holder of one of what can only be called three hereditary knighthoods which have existed in Ireland since the fourteenth century. Although the knighthoods are hereditary they do not carry the title of 'Sir' which seems very fitting in the case of this certainly curious Irish title. The present holder of the Knighthood of Glin is Mr. Desmond John Villiers Fitz-Gerald, 29th Knight of Glin, of Glin Castle, co. Limerick. In addition to the Glin knighthood there is that of the Knight of Kerry, held by the Baronet, Sir Arthur Henry Brinsley Fitz-Gerald who is the 22nd Knight of Kerry. There was also the White Knight, the first of whom was Sir Gilbert Fitzjohn Fitz-Gerald, but his line died out in the seventeenth century in the male line.

No really satisfactory explanation of this curious title exists. Sir Bernard Burke stated that the three hereditary knighthoods were created by John FitzThomas Fitz-Gerald Lord of Decies and Desmond, by virtue of his royal seigniory as Count Palatine. But other authorities, Betham and Russell state that the knights were so created by King Edward III at the battle of Hallidon Hill, 19th July, 1333. There is no definite conclusion to the controversy on this subject, but the Knights have been styled as such in Acts of Parliament, in patents under the Great Seal, and in legal proceedings. The full ancestry of this family will be found under the title of the Duke of Leinster, in *Burke's Peerage*, together with that of the line of the Knights of Kerry (Baronets) and in *Burke's Landed Gentry of Ireland*, under Fitz-Gerald, the Knight of Glin.

134. What is a Count Palatine?

In England there are no native counts, the title count never having been able to supersede that of earl, but the influence of count is shown in the term county, which exists alongside the old English shire. Now a count palatine was a great earl who had within the area over which he ruled the same powers as those of the sovereign, these being of course granted or conceded to him by the latter. Earldoms of this type did exist in England before the Norman Conquest, and indeed the great earls who ruled over vast tracts in England were often in a position of strength *vis-à-vis* the king which enabled them to dominate him. William the Conqueror was determined that such mighty subjects should not exist under his règime, but even he had to grant considerable powers to two of his nobles. One of these was the Earl of Chester and the other was the Prince Bishop of Durham. It must be clearly understood that the term Count Palatine or Bishop Palatine was not used or known in England before 1066, and that such terms, like those of duke, or marquess, viscount or baron, are importations from the continent. The Earl of Chester had the task of watching and guarding what was in effect the western frontier of England against the incursions of the Welsh who despite all efforts of either Saxon or Norman kings remained independent until the conquest of Wales under Edward I in 1284. The ruler of the dangerous area of Durham had likewise the task of facing the Scots, but here the title of Palatine was given to a churchman. On the continent there were many prince bishops in the Middle Ages, and as churchmen they could not have legitimate heirs, hence they were not so likely to try to build up a semi-dynastic position as against the king. John Selden, the greatest writer in English on titles, and whose grave can now be seen in the rebuilt Temple Church in London, writes of the Bishop of Durham that the seals of the Bishops showed on one side 'a Bishop sitting in his chair, and on the other an armed man on horseback, his sword drawn, and the Bishop's arms sometimes of his family, sometimes of his bishoprick on the shield circumscribed with the like words (i.e. *Dei gratia Episcopus Dunelmensis*, by the grace of God, Bishop of Durham), which shape on the reverse is expressed, *tanquam Comitis Palatini*, as of a count Palatine'. Selden, *Titles of Honour* (Second Part, Chapter V, s.8). Selden also refers to the ancient Earls of Pembroke as being Earls or Counts Palatine, from the fact that they dealt with the sometime dangerous country of South Wales. In Ireland it would be quite natural for a great Anglo-Norman nobleman to have palatine jurisdiction, but all such jurisdictions lapsed with the progress of government throughout England, Wales and Ireland.

135. What other Irish titles are there?

While the title of the three hereditary Knights mentioned in answer to question 133 is of English origin, there are quite a number of titles in Ireland which correspond to those of the Scottish Highlands. Among them may be reckoned such famous titles as those of O'Conor Don, MacGillicuddy of the Reeks, O'Donoghue of the Glens, O'Grady of Killyballowen, O'Donovan of Clan Cathal, MacDermot of Coolavin, and many others. Most of these are descended from the ancient kings of the Irish provinces, and sometimes from the High Kings of Ireland. The style of 'The' is used before their names in most references to them, and their wives are usually styled Madame. In Thom's *Directory of Ireland*, there will be found a list of chieftaincies whose titles have been investigated by the Chief Herald of Ireland, though out of a potential seventy, only some twenty have been cleared. This is only a matter of time, however, since most of these ancient chieftaincies require only a careful genealogical examination in order to ascertain the date from which they may approximately be reckoned.

136. What are Jacobite titles?

These are titles of nobility created by the princes of the House of Stuart after their exile to the continent in the reign of James II. The latter was held by the British Parliament to have abdicated in 1688, when he left England and went to France. He created a number of honours in Ireland during his time there, 1689–90. Among these were the titles of Marquess and Duke of Tyrconnel conferred on the Earl of Tyrconnel; that of Lord Fitton of Gawsworth on Sir

Alexander Fitton; of Baron of Bophin on Col. John Burke and several others. In addition to this there were patents of nobility made out afterwards by James II, and by his son the Old Pretender (known to many sentimental persons even now as James III, and even so styled by Prof. Trevelyan), and his grandson, the Young Pretender, Bonnie Prince Charlie. There is a large work on this interesting subject, by the late Marquis de Ruvigny, *The Jacobite Peerage*, 1904. None of these titles was recognized by the Government or Court of Great Britain.

137. Is it true that the legitimate heir to the British throne exists in the line of the Kings of Bavaria?

No, the legitimate and lawful heir to the British throne is Her Majesty, Queen Elizabeth II. It is amazing to me that there should be people, even officers who have served in the armed forces and who have presumably taken an oath of loyalty to Her Majesty or her predecessors, who can still talk about the Stuarts as being the legitimate heirs of the kingdom. The Stuart family had proved themselves to be an enormous nuisance to the country and were sent off in favour of a sovereign, descended from James I of England, but who would agree to uphold the law and religion of the country as established by Parliament. I have known men who have written about ancestors or connections of theirs as having served in 'the Hanoverian army' meaning the British army in the eighteenth century. This is of course rubbish, and not even sentimental rubbish at that.

For those who like to trace genealogies, it can be said that the present representative of the Stuarts in the female line is Albert, Duke of Bavaria, son of Crown Prince Rupert, the eldest son of Maria Theresa of Modena and of Ludwig III, formerly King of Bavaria. This line of descent comes from the fifth daughter of Charles I, Henrietta, who married the Duke of Orleans and who lived from 1644 to

1670. The line is traced through the Kings of Sardinia into the family of the Kings of Bavaria. It must have been a little awkward for those who still cherished some vague Jacobitism to realize that in the war of 1914–18 they were opposed by Prince Rupert (Rupprecht) of Bavaria, their 'rightful' king.

The male line of the Stuarts became extinct with Henry Stuart, Cardinal York, who died in 1807. He sent his royal jewels to the British sovereign, George III, and in the view of some Scottish Jacobites this constituted George III as the tanistair of Henry, in other words, the heir to the royal line appointed by the last of the male line. By this means it has become possible for Scottish Jacobites to write offensively about George I and George II, but to accept subsequent Hanoverian sovereigns as legitimate.

The Houses of Stuart and Hanover were of course cousins, since both descended from James I. Hence too the term Jacobite, from Jacobus, James.

138. What is the proper title of Queen Elizabeth – I or II?

I include this question, although it ought not to require an answer, in deference to Scots, some of whom put this question to me when I was lecturing at Inverness in 1953. The correct title is of course, Elizabeth II. The matter was discussed in Parliament at the time of Her Majesty's accession, and follows on the principle which prevailed in 1901 when Edward VII became king. In neither his case nor that of the present Queen has there been a sovereign of Scotland with the name respectively of Edward or Elizabeth, but since the union of the two countries, in 1707, as Great Britain, the numerals employed in England have given the principle of numbering the sovereigns of the United Kingdom. Numerous instances can be cited from the history of Europe that show the practice has often prevailed in foreign countries of following the numeration of one country after a union of two lands rather than starting a new series of numbers. Thus with the union of France and Navarre, in 1589, the line of succeeding kings followed the numeration already used in France. The Kings of Prussia when they became Emperors of Germany carried on with the same numeration which they had already used.

Objection to the title of Queen Elizabeth II is an example of nationalist feeling. No doubt objection to it will continue in Scottish sentiment, and occasional instances be seen of the II being crossed out on the Queen's portraits and photographs, and substituted by I.

139. Who is Black Rod?

His full title is Gentleman Usher of the Black Rod, and he ranks high among the officials of the Court, coming under the Lord Chamberlain. His name or title comes from the ebony stick which he carries as his badge of office and which is surmounted by a gold lion. His office dates from the foundation of the Order of the Garter in 1348, and he is the usher of that Order. He attends for the most part upon Parliament, and one of his chief duties is to bear messages from the House of Lords to the House of Commons. When he goes ceremonially to the House of Commons, the door is always slammed in his face, and he must then knock and announce his errand. The reason for this is that once King Charles I went down to the House of Commons to arrest five members whom he regarded as obnoxious to him, and from that time no sovereign has entered the Commons.

140. Why cannot the sovereign enter the House of Commons?

For the reason given at the end of the answer to question 139. I may add, however, that it would hardly ever have been likely that the sovereign would want to be present in the Commons. The two houses began to be spoken of as separate bodies from the end of the fourteenth century, and it seems that earlier than that they had begun to sit in separate chambers. Thus arose the practice of the sovereign summoning the Commons to the bar of the House of Lords to hear the Gracious Speech from the Throne. As I have pointed out elsewhere (in my book, *Ramshackledom*), the whole procedure of the Queen's opening of Parliament is an elaborate play, anachronistically staged, to take the on-lookers back to the days when monarchy ruled as well as reigned in this country. The Prime Minister stands at the bar of the Lords listening to the sovereign reading the speech which he has written for her. It looks just as though the situation of 500 or more years back were still true, and that the sovereign ruled, while the Lords occupy a very much more important place than the Commons. In fact of course all the roles in actuality are reversed.

It is true that when the House of Commons was rebuilt, the late King George VI went over the building to look at it, before any sitting took place. It is also true that the members of the royal house can sit in the special gallery listening to speeches in the Commons, and it is a fact that as late as Queen Anne, the sovereign would sit incognito in the gallery of the Lords listening to debates which often touched closely upon her views and policies.

141. What is the difference between the office of Lord Great Chamberlain and that of Lord Chamberlain?

The Lord Great Chamberlain is one of the Great Officers of State. He holds a position of some considerable responsibility, in that he is concerned with the management of the Houses of Parliament, and especially on great ceremonial occasions such as the state opening of Parliament. The Houses of Parliament meet by the sovereign's permission in the Palace of Westminster, and therefore it is fitting that an officer of the sovereign should administer the Palace. The office of Lord Great Chamberlain became hereditary in the family of De Vere who were Earls of Oxford. On the failure of this family in the male line, the office passed to the representatives in the female line, so that the office alternates between the Earls of Ancaster and the Marquesses of Cholmondeley. Thus the Earl of Ancaster held the office in the reign of George VI, and the Marquess of Cholmondeley in the reign of Edward VIII and at present in the reign of Elizabeth II. The Lord Chamberlain has many more duties than those of the Lord Great Chamberlain. The latter has been superseded in many important duties by the Lord Chamberlain. The duties of Lord Chamberlain are many and varied. He deals with the applications of all those who wish to attend Court, and although Courts in the sense that debutantes are presented at them no longer exist, there is still a great deal for the Lord Chamberlain to do in connection with the Palace Garden Parties, and the Royal Enclosure at Ascot. Then there is the matter of the Diplomatic Corps. Although the Lord Chamberlain works through the Marshal of the Diplomatic Corps, he still has to be ultimately responsible for the ceremonial which is observed at the reception of ambassadors at the Court of St. James. For just as we observe the form of opening of Parliament by the sovereign which prevailed centuries ago, so all ambassadors must present their credentials to the Queen at her Court of St. James's. This applies although the actual reception takes place at Buckingham Palace whither the state landau conducts the new ambassador.

In addition the duties of the Lord Chamberlain include the appointment of the royal warrant holders, one of the most closely hedged about of all royal privileges. It is hard to obtain the royal warrant, but easy to lose it by some flaw in conduct, or by the death of the holder for the warrant is always a personal matter. The Lord Chamberlain also appoints the Poet Laureate, and the Master of the Queen's Music. He is responsible for the licensing of plays. This comes within his scope because there was an old office known as that of Master of the Revels which was transferred to the Lord Chamberlain. It therefore happens that every play must be licensed by the Lord Chamberlain.

142. What is the difference between *Burke* and *Debrett*?

I have often been asked this question, and although my service with peerage works has been exclusively with *Burke,* I think that I can answer it without undue bias. Both books deal with the peerage, but while *Debrett* is concerned largely with biography, of the living, *Burke* is equally concerned with the dead, and their biographies. In other words *Debrett* is biographical, *Burke* is genealogical or concerned with family history. Both works are essential to a proper comprehension of our titled system and for reference to our notables, but no one who is primarily concerned with genealogy is likely to use *Debrett* in preference to *Burke.*

143. Why do some princes have the title of Serene Highness?

The answer to this question goes very far back into the Middle Ages, in fact right to the later period of the Roman Empire. Serene derives from *serenitas,* and there were other titles of a similar nature such as Excellentissimus, Illustrissimus and Celsitudo (the last could be literally 'Highness'). In the course of time as medieval Europe climbed out of the dark ages, these forms of title became applicable to great personages who were yet not of the ranks of kings. The most august ruler who bore the title of Serene was the Doge of Venice, known always as The Most Serene. In our time, the Prince of Monaco is His Serene Highness.

144. What was the practice known as 'touching for the King's Evil'?

This practice arose from the habits of life of St. Edward the Confessor. The latter as anyone can see who takes the trouble to read Shakespeare's *Macbeth*, was believed to possess the power to work miracles. There seems to have been great evidence for this, from the early lives of the saint. It was further thought that he would bequeath this power to his successors. At least the practice developed from this and it was not until the time of William of Orange that there was a break in the continuity of the practice. Queen Anne resumed it, and one of the last to be touched by her was the famous Dr. Samuel Johnson, when a small child. The 'King's Evil' was particularly skin disease or nervous disorder.

145. Who is the High Constable of Scotland?

This is the holder of the earldom of Erroll, which can pass through the female as well as the male line. At present the hereditary Lord High Constable of Scotland is the Countess of Erroll, the 23rd holder of the title. She is the 27th hereditary High Constable of Scotland, and in virtue of her position she has the right of precedence over all other hereditary honours and next to the royal family. This position has been acknowledged during the state visits of George IV, Edward VII, George V and Elizabeth II. The Constable has the right of presiding over the Court of the Verge, with jurisdiction of all matters of assault and riot within four miles of the sovereign's person when the latter is in Scotland. These rights were preserved in the Treaty of Union in 1707 between England and Scotland, and also in the Act of 1747 for the abolition of Hereditable Jurisdictions. In addition the Earl or Countess of Erroll together with the Earl of Angus (the Duke of Hamilton) are the hereditary Lords Assessors in the Court of the Lord Lyon. A sitting of this Court was held during the time of the 6th International Congress of Heraldry and Genealogy in 1962 in Edinburgh, when the two assessors sat with the Lord Lyon to hear a case.

146. Is there an office of Lord High Constable in England?

Yes, but the appointment is made only for a particular time, this being for the Coronation, *pro hac vice.* In 1953 the holder of the office was Viscount Alanbrooke, who died in 1963. Until the time of Henry VIII the office was hereditary and held for life, then passing to the next heir. It came into the family of Stafford, Dukes of Buckingham, but the 3rd Duke of Buckingham fell a victim to the jealousy of Henry VIII, egged on by the machinations of Cardinal Wolsey. With his execution, the appointment of Lord High Constable ceased to be a permanency, it being alleged that it was dangerous for one man to have the command of the whole of the forces of the kingdom, and to be able to pass this on to his son. For the duty of the Constable was to command the royal army. Henceforth, the post would only be temporary and would in fact last only for the coronation period, being also only ceremonial in its function.

147. Who is the Earl Marshal?

The Duke of Norfolk, who is hereditary Earl Marshal. This position he holds from a patent of 1672 which gave to his ancestor the 6th Duke of Norfolk, the office of Earl Marshal with remainder to numerous branches of his family. Thus although the present Duke of Norfolk has no son this does not mean that the title of Duke of Norfolk will become extinct or that the Earl Marshalship will revert to the Crown, as the Duke has plenty of relatives in the male line, one of whom will inherit both the dukedom and the Earl Marshalship. The duties of Earl Marshal are partly concerned with ceremonial, at times such as a royal wedding, or a coronation; and for the rest with the management of the College of Arms.

148. Who is the hereditary Grand Falconer of England?

The Duke of St. Albans. He descends from Charles II and Nell Gwynn. It was to the first Duke, his bastard son, that Charles II granted the position of Master Falconer, and also Registrar of the Court of Chancery. Neither of these offices is now exercised by the holder. Falconry has ceased to be a royal pastime though still pursued by a small number of enthusiasts, in England and Wales.

149. Who was the Lord Keeper?

He was the Lord Keeper of the Great Seal and was appointed by letters patent. He was the equal of the Lord High Chancellor, but the last Lord Keeper was Sir Robert Henley who became Lord Chancellor in 1760.

150. What is the office of the Lord High Chancellor?

He is the head of the legal system of England and Wales, and in addition is the Speaker of the House of Lords. He is the keeper of the Great Seal. He was originally the secretary of the sovereign, and his office can be traced to the reign of Edward the Confessor (1042–1066). Through the office of the Chancellor there developed the peculiar English legal device of equity, whereby cases which could not be satisfactorily solved by common law, were cleared by recourse to the sovereign, access being through the court of the Chancellor. As late as 1876 there were still the two systems of law, one of equity, the other of common law. They were then merged, with proviso that in case of conflict the rules of equity were to prevail. Until that time there had been two Lords Chief Justice, one of the Common Pleas, the other of the King's (or Queen's) Bench. The latter was known as the Lord Chief Justice of England; the former post was abolished at the merger of equity and law. The

Lord Chancellor advises the Crown in the appointment of judges, except in the case of the Lord Chief Justice.

151. What is the Board of Green Cloth?

This picturesquely named body is a relic of the past which formerly had powers somewhat on the lines of the Court of the Verge (see question 145 and answer). There were also other courts within the jurisdiction of the Lord Steward who presides over the Board of Green Cloth. Nowadays the Board is concerned with the examination of the accounts of the royal household. The name of the Board is derived from the green covered table at which its business was formerly transacted.

152. Who is the Lord Steward of the Household?

The Duke of Hamilton is the Lord Steward. His symbol of office is a white staff which he receives from the sovereign personally. His appointment is not political but in the peculiar manner in which everything is conducted in England, his name like that of the Lord Chamberlain is submitted by the Premier to the sovereign.

153. Who is Master of the Horse?

The Duke of Beaufort. His duties consist in the management of the royal stables, hounds, kennels, and mews, etc. The actual detailed work is carried out by the Crown Equerry.

154. What is the office of Lord High Steward?

This is not to be confused with that of the Lord Steward. Until the passing into law of the Criminal Justice Act of 1948, it was the privilege of peers when charged with felony to be tried by their peers. At such a trial a Lord High Steward was appointed by a royal commission to preside, and he would be in fact the Lord Chancellor. The ceremonial of trying a peer by his peers was impressive but somewhat long drawn out and expensive.

155. Who is the Queen's Champion?

This is John Lindley Marmion Dymoke, whose title is The Honourable the Queen's Champion and Standard Bearer of England. This office is hereditary in the family of Dymoke which appear to have inherited the right and privilege from their predecessors, the Marmions. Previously it was the custom for the Champion to ride into Westminster Hall at the Coronation Banquet and to challenge anyone who denied the sovereign's right to the throne to single combat. There is an account of this ceremony in Sir Walter Scott's *Redgauntlet*, though there is no record in history, as there is in the romance, of anyone taking up the Champion's glove. Since the time of George IV (1820) no Coronation Banquet has been held, and hence no appearance of a Champion, but in lieu the Champion has borne the Standard of England at the Coronation.

156. Who is the Standard Bearer for Scotland?

The Earl of Dundee, better known perhaps as Mr. Scrymgeour-Wedderburn, who proved his claim to be 11th Earl of Dundee on the 18th May, 1953. As far back as 1298 Sir Alexander Scrymgeour received from Sir William Wallace the right to bear the standard of Scotland. This had previously been the privilege of the Bannerman family. At Bannockburn, Sir Alexander's son, Nicholas Scrymgeour bore the royal standard. The circumstances in which the earldom of Dundee was regained by the present earl are among the most romantic in the annals of the peerage, the title having been 'out' of his family for over 250 years.

157. Who is Lord President of the Council?

This office consists in the management of the Privy Council. The latter body antedates Parliament, or at least the House of Commons. It was the original organ of government under the early sovereigns after the Norman Conquest, and indeed a Great Council functioned for centuries before the Conquest, though under the name of the Witan. Today the appointment is a political one, and the holder is a Cabinet Minister. The Privy Council's work has been largely taken over by various ministries, but it still has work to do in the issuing of Orders in Council, and through its judicial committee, which hears appeals from certain lower courts, though with the granting of independence to the former colonial empire, the volume of appeals to the Privy Council from abroad has greatly lessened.

158. Who is the Lord Privy Seal?

This office dates from the fourteenth century when it was created in order to provide a greater safeguard to the use of public money by the sovereign. The Privy Seal had to be given in order for the Lord Chancellor to be able to affix the Great Seal to documents, and to allow the expenditure of money from the treasury. The Lord Privy Seal is quite often a Minister without portfolio or departmental duties, but usually with extra duties of a very onerous nature. It was the late J. H. Thomas who, during his tenure of the office, was asked what were his duties, and who replied that he did not know the meaning of the term, but that it did mean a lot of damned hard work.

117

159. Is the position of the Prince of Wales to be properly described as an office?

No. There is no office of Prince of Wales. If there had been such an office, it would hardly have been possible for Queen Victoria to have kept her heir, later King Edward VII in ignorance of state papers and state business for the bulk of his life until his accession to the throne. The Prince of Wales is a title and nothing more. It is conferrable only when the sovereign decides that his or her eldest son shall have the title, and be created Prince of Wales.

160. How many Orders of Chivalry are there now in the United Kingdom and Commonwealth?

There are four Orders which are obsolescent. They are, the Order of St. Patrick, to which no appointment has been made since 1922; and three Orders connected with the former Indian Empire, namely, the Order of the Star of India, the Order of the Indian Empire, and the Order of the Crown of India. To none of these three has any appointment been made since 1947.

Leaving these four on one side, we have six Orders which confer a title and two which do not. The six are: The Order of the Garter; the Order of the Thistle; the Order of the Bath; the Order of St. Michael and St. George; the Royal Victorian Order; and the Order of the British Empire. The recipients of these honours, if made Knights of the Orders are given the prefix 'Sir' before their names.

In addition we have the Order of Merit and the Order of the Companions of Honour. These confer no title, but holders are able to add the letters, O.M., or C.H. after their names.

161. Are titles ever bought today?

I would say, no. I would also add that not very long ago

118

there was a traffic in honours. Those who are curious on the subject may care to read the book about the life of Maundy Gregory, entitled *Honours for Sale, the Strange Story of Maundy Gregory.* This is by Gerald MacMillan, It details as much as is ever likely to be known of the operations between 1922 and 1932 of the late Maundy Gregory, who was reputed to possess an income of some £30,000 per year from his ability to introduce into the right quarters the names of those who wished to receive honours.

It should be added that the history of the sale of honours begins in the reign of James I, who hit upon the expedient of getting money by selling peerages and baronetcies, sometimes upon a sort of commission basis; on one occasion he gave a blank patent of nobility to his favourite Buckingham, who then proceeded to fill in the name of the person to be 'honoured' after of course having extracted from the latter a large sum of money for his services.

Owing to the trial and sentencing of Maundy Gregory for his much lesser efforts in the field of honour begetting, the sale of honours was brought to an abrupt end. 'Sale' in the sense of large donations to charities or to party funds may continue but can hardly be classed with the activities of honour mongers.

Index

Index

DATE DUE			
MAY 6 1975			
DEC 17 1975			
MAY 24 1976	DEC 1 1 1988		
OCT 18 1977			
NOV 8 1977			
MAY 5 1979			
NOV 17 1979			
AUG 18 1981			
MAR 12 1982			
JUN 22 1982			